HOW TO STAY SOBER

A Practical Guide to Overcome Alcoholism and Drug Addiction

Dr. Emmanuel Nzuzu (PhD, MSc, MS, LMHC, CAP)

Absolute Author
Publishing House

How to Stay Sober
Copyright 2020 by Dr. Emmanuel Nzuzu (Ph.D., MSc, MS, LMHC, CAP)
ALL RIGHTS RESERVED

Publisher: Absolute Author Publishing House
Publishing Editor: Dr. Melissa Caudle
Editor: Rugare Mareva (Ph.D.)
Junior Editor: Paul S. Dupre

LIBRARY OF CONGRESS IN-PUBLICATION-DATA

How to Stay Sober/ Dr. Emmanuel Nzuzu.

ISBN Paperback: 978-1-64953-157-5
ISBN Hardback: 978-1-64953-189-6
ISBN eBook: 978-1-64953-158-2
ISBN Workbook: 978-1-64953-159-9

1.   Self-help   2. Sobriety   3. Alcoholism

Table of Contents

Foreword
By Dr. Melissa Caudle

For me, I never understood what an alcoholic was growing up; I thought that was how all dads behaved. I never saw my dad without a beer or a martini in his hand—that's what dads do, right? Well, not all dads, I soon discovered as I grew into a teen. I realized my dad had a drinking problem, and now I knew why it always bothered my mother. His drinking caused our family a great deal of pain; several times, we lost everything, including our home, because of his addiction. One would think I would never pick up an alcoholic beverage in my life because of this. Think again, I did, and for about eight years, I almost ruined my life. I was drinking every day—mind it, not at work, but at night the moment I walked in the door. No one could have talked me out of it. It took me, saying, "Enough is enough." I don't regret that decision, and now as I look back on my life, I'm elated I put that bottle down forever. Was it easy? No! The easy part came when I became a better mother, wife, friend, employee—a better person.

I don't want to lecture to anyone for any reason. However, if you are an alcoholic and want to stay sober, take the next step. You can find help, and you aren't alone. The good news, you are already on your way by reading this book "How to Stay Sober." Don't look back and blame yourself or anyone else; look forward and make your path toward sobriety and staying that way. You can do it. Seek the professional help you need because you can't do it alone.

Dr. Melissa Caudle

Bestselling Author
CEO Absolute Author Publishing House
EZBOOKBLASTER.COM

Introduction

Over the years, I have seen many alcoholics and drug addicts move in and out of treatment programs without overcoming alcohol and drugs. A lot of them go back to drinking and drug abuse soon after being discharged from a program. Many may have been attending AA/NA (Alcoholics Anonymous/Narcotics Anonymous) meetings but then slid backward by missing them. Some may have attended 90 meetings in 90 days, but the miracle didn't happen. Alcoholics and drug addicts who seek help are usually at the bottom of the bottom. They are often shattered and miserable, expressing messages of hopelessness, helplessness, and despair. They are at their weakest point in life, the lowest end of their very long addiction rope, and they usually say, "I don't know why I keep doing this to myself. I have tried everything, and nothing has worked so far. I was sober for a while but made a mistake and relapsed. I don't want to die. My loved ones don't trust me anymore. I am isolated and alone. I don't know what to do. I need help."

I wrote this book for people who desire to be sober but have run out of their options. It is a guide to those people who believe that they have tried everything, but nothing works.

Chapter 1 opens with a bold declaration that recovery is possible and always available. The primary ingredients for sobriety are motivation, a clear vision, and a willingness to be honest. Recovery is possible when you need it and seek it from inside the heart. Sobriety will not come to you, and no one can deliver it to you except yourself. You can live a life free from alcohol and drugs, but you have to cherish the new life and give up the old one. Your willingness and commitment to becoming brutally honest with yourself are critical to a successful recovery. A desire without the willingness to change will remain that, a desire, and nothing else.

Chapter 2 is appropriately titled "Self-Diagnosis." Successful recovery requires you to develop a clear, accurate, and correct understanding of the problem of alcohol and drug addiction. Progress in sobriety is experienced when the alcoholic and drug addict is persuaded and convinced beyond doubt that he/she has a problem. This is a critical issue when considering that for many years, people use alcohol and drugs accompanied by problems but do nothing or very little about it. The persuasion and convincing must come from none other than the addicted person himself/herself because the addiction disease works best through self-diagnosis. It will assist you in how to make a thorough, honest, and accurate self-diagnosis.

Chapter 3 is more about the problem; thus, the title. Once you have completed a self-diagnosis and comprehend that the problem is not alcohol or cocaine, but you are powerless over these substances. Chapter 3 discusses the consequences of powerlessness. It makes it increasingly difficult to run your life properly. When you are powerless, everything seems to go wrong, ranging from your health, relationship with yourself, legal, finances, career, marriage, and other important components of your life.

Chapter 4 covers the solution and power within yourself to overcome addiction. You have completed your self-diagnosis and have so far established what the problem is. This chapter focuses on the solution. The problem is powerlessness over alcohol and drugs. The solution to powerlessness is power, and nothing else will do. Any other solution will not give you the power necessary to abstain from alcohol and drugs. Moving to another city will not do it. Changing from whisky to wine will not do it either. Only drinking after working hours or on weekends will not work either as well. Changing your job or divorcing your current spouse will not help you stay sober. The question is, where do you get that power? This is what chapter 4 will help you answer.

Chapter 5 is the final chapter and examines the contribution of self toward the addiction process. Self is the mindset that "I want what I want now. It's either my way or no way." Your best efforts have not helped you to stay sober. Your self has failed, and you must give it up, or else you continue drinking and doing drugs, driven by selfish, self-centered, and self-seeking motives. Spiritual life starts with surrendering, whereby you admit being powerless, helpless, and that you don't know how to resolve the situation on your own. If you knew, you would have been sober long ago.

CHAPTER ONE

Recovery is Possible and Always Available

What is it to recover? It is to get back, restore, or some form of rescue. What are some things that an alcoholic and drug user would want to get back? The list includes jobs, relationships, marriage, peace of mind, getting back your good health, restoring your normal functioning, for example, going to sleep at night, waking up in the morning, going to work, getting back the habit of spending money on things that support you rather than those that ruin your life (rent, food, mortgage, clothes, transport, and vacation). Recovery is being rescued from yourself since the alcoholic, and drug addict is his/her own worst enemy by practicing selfishness, self-centeredness, and self-sabotaging habits. One needs to restore healthy hobbies and interests addiction displaced. Recovery is the restoration of all the intangible assets taken away by alcohol and drugs, such as your lost dignity, integrity, honor, self-worth, self-control, self-discipline, responsibility, love, and trust. Work in recovery will also focus on repairing broken relationships, moving from the chaos and disorder of alcoholism and drugs into a safe and structured environment where you can grow and flourish. It is challenging to have a new life if you remain in the same mental and dysfunctional emotional environment you operated in when you were abusing drugs and alcohol.

Recovery is possible when you need it and seek it from inside the heart. Sobriety will not come to you, and no one can deliver it to you except yourself. You can live a life free from alcohol and drugs, but you have to cherish the new life and give up the old one. Your willingness and commitment to becoming brutally honest with yourself are critical to a successful recovery. A desire without the willingness to change will remain that, a desire, and nothing else.

There is a right and wrong way to stop abusing drugs and alcohol and staying sober. The right path is a process of change, with an appropriate starting point, followed by interconnected activities flowing in a logical sequence. The result is progressive sobriety and restoration of normal day to day functioning throughout your recovery and beyond. To experience long-term sober living, you need to begin from the correct departure point. Some alcoholics and drug addicts talk sobriety on the outside while harboring secret and powerful desires to continue abusing drugs and alcohol. They may say things they consider being what family members expect to hear while holding hidden intentions to partake in more alcohol and drugs. Such double standards will take you nowhere, besides repeated relapses.

What is Your Motivation to Give Up Alcohol and Drugs?

Why were you so effective as an alcoholic or drug user? Success in any area of life requires motivation and a certain level of commitment. You became an expert at drinking and drug abuse because you had a powerful motivation to do it.

Your parents can push you or your husband, wife, employer, friends, teachers, and church group, but if you do not feel motivated and committed to change, it will not happen. You excelled in using alcohol and drugs because you had motivation and commitment. AA and NA meetings and rehab programs are full of unmotivated alcoholics and drug addicts who operate in both worlds, wanting to quit and wanting to use at the same time. They entertain a desire to be sober, accompanied by a secret desire not to give up alcohol and drugs. Motivation can rescue you from the struggle of having one leg in sobriety and the other in addiction. Your strong motivation to abuse intoxicating substances always prompted you to get a drink or a drug. You thought about it all day, every day, you felt it; you tasted it; you smelled it, and you promptly acted on your thoughts. Identifying your true underlying reasons for quitting alcohol and drugs will propel you to action. Your addiction to alcohol and drugs worked so well because you had your own sound reasons to indulge in them day after day. What is your real reason to do a sober life? How strong is that reason for you to change?

Successful recovery demands you identify your genuine reasons to want it. What is the valid and strong reason that makes you want to quit? Any fake, shallow, and artificial excuses will not help you. You may say that you want sobriety for your children, spouse, or some other family member. Your loved ones were always there when you were deep in your addiction. Why do you think you love and care for them so much that you are now willing to give up alcohol and drugs for them suddenly? Self-deception might have worked when you were abusing alcohol and drugs, but it won't help you get sober. You were not drinking and abusing drugs for anyone else's benefit except for yourself.

Why do you think you will quit for someone else other than yourself? You may persuade yourself to think that you are getting into recovery to save your marriage and then feel like your spouse is persecuting you for being in recovery against your will. They may convince you that you are doing it for your children and yet feel like those same children are punishing you since you can no longer drink and abuse drugs as you privately wish. You should do all you can to save your marriage and take care of your children, but these two, on their own, are not always healthy and adequate drives to keep you interested, motivated, and fired up about your recovery.

Find a solid, lasting reason to want to stay sober. That reason should be powerful enough to force you into action. Your reasons to drink and abuse drugs were often so powerful that nothing could stop you once you were on them. You got impatient and edgy when you wanted a drink or drug. Nothing could stand in your way, not your loved ones, not your job, not lack of money, not even the police and the judge. When you wanted a drink and a drug, you would make sure you had them no matter the odds. What is the driving force behind your sobriety efforts? If you cannot state this clearly and expressly, your recovery progress will be slow, challenging, and demanding. Your reason to quit should inspire you to take a determined effort towards an alcohol- and drug-free life. Your desire for drugs always made you connect with your dealer. Your desire for alcohol always compelled you to go to the gas station for a six-pack. It always worked like clockwork. What is it inside you that would motivate you to want sober living and not just daydream about it?

Bring the same excitement and energy into your recovery that you had when you were drinking and abusing drugs. What is it that can compel you to quit and stay sober this time? Maybe you know you want to change and are eager to get started. Defining that personal reason will help you get on your way. You may want to change but fear that you cannot. Specifying your reason will help in reducing the fear and spring you into action. You may experience problems with alcohol and drugs but have no desire to quit; identifying your real reason to be sober will help you see a way out of your addiction cycle. As opposed to the manufactured stories, understanding the real reason to abstain will motivate you to seek help. No one looks for help if there seems to be no need for such help. As an alcoholic and drug addict, you may experience severe substance abuse problems but rarely ask for help. People around you may tell you to change, but no one else's reason will convince you to take action except your own personal reason. Sustained action comes from your motivation and not what someone else tells you. Behavior change based on what others tell you does not always stick because it lacks personal agreement and commitment.

Real-life examples of inappropriate reasons to embark on recovery include thinking that all you need is a break because *"I am not a real alcoholic. I just want to give my body some rest and I can continue anytime,"* that family members are the problem. All you need is to stop for some time to silence them, that your life would be better if people stopped bothering you about your drinking or that all you need is to slow down then go back to drinking and drug abuse after a short period of recovery.

Many people in recovery cannot clearly articulate their motivation to stop alcohol and drugs. When asked why they are in a recovery program, some addicts say, *"I don't know for sure. The fact that I am here means that I need it."* Not necessarily so because you can take the horse to the river, but you can't force him to drink. Others may say they are in recovery because *"My life, I am the problem; I need help."* Such responses are too general and meaningless and do not inspire you to take action. These responses are usually accompanied by disempowering questions such as, *"I don't know why I am doing this to myself. I have tried everything, and nothing works. I don't know what to do to stop. I need help, but I am not sure."* These may sound like nice logical things to say, but they don't motivate you to move forward. Your reason for making a recovery should prompt you into action.

Practical Exercise 1: What Is Your Motivation?

Making a recovery for your own personal reasons seems to hold more significant promise in the long term. Ask yourself empowering questions such as What do you benefit from sobriety? What is the attraction of quitting alcohol now? What does sobriety mean to you emotionally and psychologically? What does it feel like to be finally free from alcohol and drugs? What is in it for you? What is the benefit for you in a new life of sobriety compared to your old lifestyle? Why should you change now and not later? How much longer are you willing to put up with what you go through when you drink and do drugs? How much longer are you willing to continue investing your life (time and money) in a loss-making enterprise called alcoholism?

Your answers to these questions should help you clarify your motivation to be sober and put you on the right footing for recovery work. If your reason and motivation to be sober are not clear and reliable, you will swing like a pendulum from one extreme to another. Today you are excited to be sober, and tomorrow, it's not exciting anymore. Today it looks like getting sober is the best decision you ever made, and down the road, you wonder whether you made the right choice. Now you are going back and forth, from being interested in sobriety to being bored and secretly desiring to retake alcohol and drugs. This kind of trial-and-error approach to recovery will not take you to where you want to go. Clarify your motivation to be sober.

What Are Your Intention and Vision?

"Where there is no vision, the people perish..."

Once you have clarified your personal reason and motivation to do recovery work, the next important step is to develop a clear, specific vision and intent. Addiction life is like a vicious cycle that keeps on spinning and reproducing the same unwanted experiences. For much of your drinking time, you kept thinking in ways that kept you stranded in alcoholism, although it didn't look like being stagnant. However, with hindsight, you can see the wasted time and missed opportunities. You behaved in ways that strengthened your alcohol addiction habits. You made choices that led to the same pitfalls and regrets. You engaged in an endless pattern of self-defeating thoughts and beliefs and then wondered why your life was not improving. You walked in the same dreary mental and emotional paths, falling in the same ditches repeatedly without being roused from the slumber. Of course, it puzzled you why things were not working out for you, especially when alcohol and drugs became involved. You concerned yourself that you had tried and failed to straighten and effectively control alcohol use. In fact, the more you tried, the worse you felt; then failure and limited success became your dwelling place, your home, your official residence. You became preoccupied with why things were not working for you and lived in anticipation of more hardships because you couldn't move out of Point "A."

The longer you stayed in Point "A," the harder and more impossible it was for you to see a way out. You cannot get to Point "B" if you spend all day every day in Point "A." The way out is to have a clear vision and specific intent. To change successfully, you must be guided by a vision of the future and not memories of the past. The Bible refers to the fact that without a vision, people perish. You cannot see Point "B" if the whole of you is consumed by Point "A" where all things are going wrong, it's so hard, nothing works, it's impossible, you have tried and failed, you don't care anymore, and another drink would make you feel better. Your vision is your link between where you are now and your desired future sober life. It helps you shift your focus and attention from an addiction lifestyle to the ideal you have always yearned for, an alcohol-free life. Your vision takes you from what has been going wrong to what you can do right for a change.

Vision opens your eyes from focusing on the questions and problems to concentrating on the answers and solutions. You cannot see the solution if you spend most of your time crying about the problem, how dire your situation is, why everyone doesn't understand you, or how unique your case is. The only result you get from dwelling on the problem is self-pity, feeling sorry for yourself, and nothing more. Vision helps you to think outside the box, to see beyond your current limitations and past failures. Vision helps you to break up your relationship with hopelessness and helplessness. You cannot move to any new destination if all you do is discuss, describing, explaining harping on about what you don't want. Feeling sorry for yourself will not help you get sober; a clear vision will.

Practical Exercise 2: What Is Your Vision? (Where Are You Now, And Where Do You Want to Go?)

Changing from alcoholism to sober living can be likened to the transformation from Point "A" to Point "B." Describe the quality of your life at Point "A." How do you feel about yourself being at Point "A?" How would you describe your addiction life experiences at Point "A?" How many years have you been at Point "A?" How long have you been trying to get out of Point "A?" What do you say to yourself about being at Point "A" for so long? What do other people say to you about your addiction lifestyle? How do you respond to what they say? What have you tried to do so far to get out? How well have your recovery attempts worked so far? What worked, what did not work, and why? What is keeping you stuck in Point "A?"

Your vision is your Point, "B." It is your desired future of life without alcohol. It is best to see yourself experiencing that desired future life in the present moment. See yourself in that role of having successfully recovered. Success means different things to different people. What is a successful recovery for you? What is your life going to be like when you are clean and sober? How do you think, feel, and act now that you are free from alcohol? What is your new attitude? What would you say to yourself now that you are sober? (Recall what you said to yourself at the height of your addiction). How would you relate and talk to others now that you have successfully changed? How do you want to be perceived?

What is an intention, and why is it essential to have one?

Intention is knowing what you want and getting clear of what you want to do, have and be. Your intent is like a plan, an idea of what you are going to do and attain. It should be evident to you. Intention is a resolve, a determination of what you want from recovery, and it should direct your perceptions, choices, and actions. If you are intent on doing something, you are willing and determined to get it done. You have a burning desire to do it and complete it, and you have a firm belief that you can do it and achieve it; you have high expectations of your ability to do it and experience the results instantly. Intention helps you stay on task until the end, stay focused, and not allow outside distractions to derail your progress. You leave no stone unturned until you get what you want.

The above may sound straightforward and too theoretical; however, they are more complex and challenging in real life. You may say to yourself, "This is easier said than done. He doesn't know what I am going through. He doesn't know my unique problems and special situation. I have tried everything, and nothing works."

The intention process can be depicted:

Step 1: Clear Intention: I want to drink. I want to smoke weed. (These are intention statements for when you were using drugs and taking alcohol). I want to attend one AA meeting daily. I want to change from dishonesty to honesty daily, from hurting and pushing loved one's away to showing love and care daily.

Step 2: Great Expectation: As soon as you say what you want, you are automatically showing desire, expectation, belief, and anticipation. That is the desire to drink, expect to get drunk, and believe that you will get drunk no matter what, the anticipation that it's going to happen without fail, quick and soon. Getting drunk becomes the only important task, and not much else matters. Have great expectations about your sobriety intentions, just like you were having when you were drinking.

Step 3: Attention: All your attention instantly goes to getting drunk, and your energy follows your attention. You become emotionally charged and physically absorbed in getting your next drink. Pay attention, become emotionally charged about getting sober, be honest, attend your AA support group meetings, or work on any other recovery activity.

Step 4: Elevated Feelings: Your intention to drink is so clear, strong, and powerful that it arouses feel-good feelings of excitement, some thrill, desperation, and eagerness to get it done. You may even feel high before putting your hands on the alcohol or your drug of choice. Some people tell me they could smell it and taste it in their mouths just by anticipating its delivery by the dealer. You were excited and energized about going to drink and do drugs; how much anticipation and excitement do you have for your sobriety?

Step 5: Action: The elevated feelings strengthen your resolve to get the drink with no unnecessary delays. Now you can't wait. You got to get a drink. You become impatient and angry at any perceived obstacles and hindrances against fulfilling your intention to drink. What elevated emotions do you have about making a recovery and being sober? How much gratitude, joy, appreciation, and thankfulness do you have that you are sober today? If your sobriety does not give you joy and gratitude, hang on because you soon find it in alcohol and drugs. Without anticipation, expectation, excitement, and gratitude, it won't be long before you relapse.

As you can see, intending is very easy because you practiced living by intent throughout your drinking days. There was nothing that could stop you or delay you when you intended to have a drink. Your strong intent to drink left no room for failure or giving up. You never entertained failure in getting alcohol on all those times you got drunk. There was no giving up once you decided to drink. Your intention ensured you kept drinking until you got drunk. You may have fallen, but you quickly stood up and kept moving on until you got your heart's desires. You carried on until you fulfilled your drinking wishes. This is the same intention that you should bring to your recovery work.

No obstacle could stand in your way when you wanted alcohol or a drug. Lack of money was never an issue because your intention was so firm that you always had a way to get both the money and the alcohol or sometimes alcohol with no money. Time was never a constraint because you always had more than enough time for alcohol and drugs. Other things could wait, but not alcohol. Family responsibilities and work commitments could not prevent you from drinking because alcohol was a priority. The mere thought of alcohol would excite you and make you jump into action, driven by heightened anticipation of the next drink. You thought about alcohol from sunrise to sunset. You were preoccupied with it all day, every day. Can you bring the same energy and excitement to your recovery work?

Give life to your intention by attaching an elevated emotion. Heightened emotions of joy, excitement, expectation, sense of relief, and anticipation gave life and vitality to your intention to drink. The elevated feelings energized your desires to drink. How much energy are you investing in your sobriety? How expectant, anticipatory, and excited are you about your recovery work so far? How excited are you about being sober today? How much joy, expectation, and anticipation do you have about another day without alcohol? How thankful are you about Friday nights and weekends that are free from alcohol and drugs? How satisfied and secure do you feel about being able to go out and come back with all your money because you no longer drink?

Intention without emotion is lifeless. When you were drinking, you had confidence, determination, and self-assurance about drinking alcohol. You gave energy to intentions to get high by the emotions you had for alcohol. What emotions do you have about recovery? How do you feel about giving up alcohol? How do you feel about spending your Friday nights and weekends away from your favorite drinking places? How excited are you about spending the holidays and the rest of your life doing other things besides alcohol and drugs?

Put life and vitality to your sober intentions by attaching elevated positive emotions into your recovery work. That includes being thankful you are out of the fog and can think and concentrate clearly for a change, being in anticipation and great expectation of the next AA/NA meeting you are going to attend, being grateful and appreciative that you can hang out with friends and family, which was not happening before because of alcohol. Initially, this may look hard and impossible because you are not used to having sober intentions and empowering emotions of gratitude, appreciation, and joy. Remember that you didn't become a veteran addict on day one; you kept drinking until you became an alcoholic. So, it is with your sober intentions and the elevated emotions that should go with it. Keep doing it day after day, and the magic will happen.

Unfortunately, you may say that you want to be sober but immediately tell yourself that it's hard, it's impossible, you cannot do it, you have tried and failed, it doesn't work, nothing works. You were bold with alcohol but weak and helpless with your sobriety. You were more engaged and aggressive with alcohol, but relatively subdued and unenthusiastic about your sobriety. You were carefree when you were drinking but impose conditions to your recovery. You want to be sober, but you don't want to lose your drinking buddies. You don't want to give up the joy and pleasures of intoxication. The intention is, "I want to be sober," followed by empowering questions such as:

- What does sobriety mean to you?
- How would you feel when you are sober?
- What do you do to occupy yourself when you are sober? What is it like to be sober?

The more you answer these questions, the clearer and distinct the images of sobriety you have, and that is your intention.

Future vs. Past Orientation: Stop Living in the Past

Intention is enormously powerful. You drank alcohol and used drugs by intention. It doesn't matter whether you were aware of it. It doesn't matter whether you believe it. Every time you went to drink and pass out, the intention was there with you. You intended to experience the same sense of ease and comfort that alcohol gave you in previous days. You intended to chase the high that cocaine always delivered. You intended to numb the painful feelings, a vital service which alcohol always provided on demand. Your intentions were always past- and not future-oriented. You wanted to drink today and feel the way it felt like yesterday. You were using yesterday's experiences as a reference point for dealing with today's circumstances and challenges. You repeated past drinking behaviors because you got used to the familiar, the known, which looks natural, real, and more like who you are being.

In order to change, your intentions should have a future orientation and be in alignment with your vision. Your new life is not in the known. Sobriety is not something you are used to and feels good. Sober life is in the unknown, and it feels strange, unreal, and uncomfortable. Your sober intentions should support and complement your vision and not contradict it. Your intention should keep you focused on the new life and not the unwanted familiar past from where you are coming. Your obvious intentions should keep you preoccupied with what you want and not what you don't want, what you have and not what you don't have, what you like and not what you don't like. It's easy for a recovering addict to become consumed by what is wrong, what is not working, how hard things are, how everyone doesn't understand and like you, and blame, blame. Keeping your eyes on your sober intentions should help you appreciate the number of days you have been sober, be grateful you are still alive and well, that you didn't die on all those occasions that death could have happened.

When you wanted to drink alcohol, your mind immediately started producing scenarios, images, and feelings of going to the store, getting a drink, opening, and enjoying a good time. Repetition with aggressiveness, consistency, frequency, and persistency will help you stay sober. Your energy follows your attention. Whatever you pay attention to grows. Paying daily attention to your sober intention will take you closer to your vision, the desired new life free from alcohol. There are no shortcuts. There are no quick fixes. That worked with alcohol and drugs but does not work when you want to change and improve your life. Intend to achieve sobriety day after day, with elevated emotions every day. That is how you kept the addiction going, you intended it day after day, and you were very successful at being an alcoholic. This is neither hard nor impossible because you did alcohol with a lot of zeal and excitement. Pay attention to the new sober life you are creating instead of whining, blaming, complaining, and regretting. What is wrong is always inside you, within you, and not outside there?

Need for Rigorous Honesty

Being very honest with yourself is essential for a life free from alcohol and drugs. Recovery is an inside job;

everything starts with you. Honesty is not just about telling the truth. It sees things as they are and not what they appear to be or what you imagine them to be. Honesty is about what you think, say, and believe about your relationship with alcohol and drugs. What you think and believe can either work for you or against you. How honest were your thoughts and beliefs about alcohol when you were using it? Honesty should promote your welfare and that of your loved ones. How well did your lifestyle of alcohol abuse promote your interests and those of your loved ones?

Alcoholic behavior is driven by self-deception and dishonesty, which is lodged in your predominant daily thought patterns, self-talk content, feelings, and perceptions that guide your drinking life. Below are some real-life examples of such self-deception and dishonesty practiced by alcoholics.

Jingo: *"It was all about me. I was completely dedicated to alcohol and nothing else. I was insensitive and inconsiderate. I harmed my innocent loved ones and felt very justified. I pushed them away but kept wondering why I was lonely, sad, and isolated. I was convinced that I cared too much, and they didn't care at all. So, I started doing things to spite them back."*

Brett: *"I sincerely believed that nobody knew what I was doing. I thought I was doing a good job of hiding the alcohol and drugs. I am disturbed and ashamed for blinding my eyes from the hard facts that were always there in the open. The world outside me saw It, but I didn't."*

Jodak: *"I thought other people were the reason I was drinking too much. I convinced myself that I didn't have a drinking problem and that no one knew what was going on in my life. I knew my drinking was not harming anyone, and I didn't understand why my loved ones were fussing so much."*

Bango: *"I would try to convince myself that everything was going on very well, but many times it was the opposite. A lot of things were going wrong when I was drinking, but I did not see it that way. I guess I was cheating myself. I now realize that I was dishonest to myself about who I was. I get nervous to discover how much I was lying to myself all these years."*

Dishonesty is believing a lie and living that lie. It is double standards; one standard for your private consumption and another one for public display. When you are dishonest, you always worry about what they are saying about you because you can't tell which version of yourself people are seeing. When you lie to yourself about who you are, you live in constant fear of exposure and may need a drink to numb the fear and anxiety aroused by self-deception. Rigorous honesty requires you to match your behaviors with your intentions that your choices and actions are in line with what you want your life to be, and how you appear is who you really are and not something else. Your daily self-talk must support your goal to be sober and not contradict it. The thoughts you hold in your inner self must help you go in the right direction and to stay on track.

Here are some helpful questions to help you assess your level of honesty when you were drinking alcohol and using drugs. Answer them honestly. There are no right or wrong answers.

1. How honest were you about your drinking lifestyle? What were the things and issues about which you were dishonest?

2. What were the consequences of dishonesty to you first and other people in your life?

3. What were the financial and emotional consequences of being dishonest?

4. List and describe five things you are going to practice, so you become rigorously honest.

Honesty is the opposite of self-deception and self-defeating thinking. Some alcoholics swear that they have always been honest, never told a lie to anyone and that they have always been open about their drinking. True, you may not have lied with your mouth, but we deliver lies through many vehicles. You may lie by omitting to tell your spouse all the places you have been. Your behavior often speaks louder than your words. For a long time, the alcoholic has perceived things, people, and situations not as they are but as he/she likes them to be. Here are some examples of dishonest thinking and behavior:

1. An alcoholic who blames the police for his DUI;
2. An alcoholic who is resentful at his ex-employer for losing his job because of alcohol and absenteeism; and,

3. Someone who has frequent blackouts, passing out, with ugly hangovers and calls this relaxing or having a good time.

The Big Book of Alcoholics Anonymous (AA) describes addicts as naturally incapable of grasping and developing a manner of living that demands rigorous honesty. Honesty is not just a word or a good idea. It is a pillar that your sobriety and recovery life must lean on. It is the bridge that you must cross to a life free from alcohol and drugs. Work at being rigorously honest because dishonesty and self-deception are at the heart of every relapse. Of course, you do not automatically become trustworthy. Work at it so you can grow in your recovery. Without this critical ingredient, relapse will be a frequent visitor to your recovery work, and you will be in and out of rehab programs.

Practical Daily Exercise 6: My Daily Recovery Success Factors

This daily self-reflection tool assists you in paying continuous attention to your vision and intentions. Please rate yourself on each of the following important daily self-check items on a scale of 1 to 10 (lowest to highest) by circling the correct number.

DAILY SELF-CHECK

Date:
Time:
Day of the Week:

1. Today, I strongly want to be sober for myself.

    1 2 3 4 5 6 7 8 9 10

2. Today, I am highly motivated to work on staying sober.

    1 2 3 4 5 6 7 8 9 10

3. Today, I strongly believe I succeed in staying sober.

    1 2 3 4 5 6 7 8 9 10

4. Today, I have strong self-confidence in staying sober.

    1 2 3 4 5 6 7 8 9 10

5. Today, I am very interested in doing all it takes to stay sober.

    1 2 3 4 5 6 7 8 9 10

6. Today, I will do all that I have to do to stay sober.

1 2 3 4 5 6 7 8 9 10

7. Today, I am very open and honest about staying sober.

1 2 3 4 5 6 7 8 9 10

8. Today, I am very grateful to be sober.

1 2 3 4 5 6 7 8 9 10

9. Today, I have great expectations about staying sober.

1 2 3 4 5 6 7 8 9 10

10. Today, I am in a very good mood concerning my sobriety.

1 2 3 4 5 6 7 8 9 10

11. Today, I have a very positive attitude toward my new life of sobriety.

1 2 3 4 5 6 7 8 9 10

What aspects of yourself need some improvement today, and what specifically are you going to do to improve those aspects?

CHAPTER TWO

Self-Diagnosis: How to Identify the Problem of Addiction to Alcohol and Drugs

Alcoholism is a disease, and many people who drink don't know that they have an illness. It is impossible to treat a disease that you don't believe you have. Now and again, an alcoholic may have a passing feeling that all is not well but is not sure what is wrong; and the drinking continues. To the alcoholic, the drinking lifestyle looks very ordinary. Everyone else drinks alcohol; besides, it is legal, although it may sometimes cause you to do illegal things. Most diseases have signs and symptoms, and many of them are for the disease of alcoholism and drug abuse. Such symptoms are often ignored by the alcoholic and drug addict. Ignorance of his/her disease is the major reason the alcoholic keeps drinking while problems pile up. Unfortunately, alcohol and drug addictions are the only diseases that a client must make a self-diagnosis. If you disagree, try to force an alcoholic to seek help or get a drug addict into a treatment program and see how much you like the response. Many addicts are court-ordered into programs but continue to use the substances while attending treatment or go back to drugs and alcohol as soon as they are discharged from the facility. For them, there is nothing wrong or unusual about using drugs while attending AA because they believe they don't have a problem. The judge and the police may be the problem, not the 'innocent' addict caught on the wrong side of the law.

There is a need for a sound understanding of the problem of alcoholism and drug use. Alcoholics and drug addicts often assume that they know the problem, yet they continue using drugs and drinking. Such contradictory behavior does not seem to reflect adequate knowledge and understanding of the real problem. There is no difference between ignorance and knowing a problem; you do nothing about it and continue to indulge. Pouring gasoline on a fire does not put out the fire but makes it bigger and worse. Continued drinking when you know you have a problem does not reduce the problem but makes it worse. The sad thing about the problem is that the alcoholic does not know the problem, although he/she claims to know. Just being aware of a problem without taking corrective action is not sufficient. Your life is an extension of your thoughts. Continuous drinking behavior and drug addiction lifestyle do not reflect a clear understanding of what you are going through. Lack of understanding of the problem is the primary reason your previous efforts to deal with alcoholism and drug addiction had limited success, if any.

Alcoholics and drug addicts who no longer enjoy using alcohol and drugs often suffer from inaction because of lack of understanding and sometimes because of complete denial. The addicted person may now and again question himself if he is an actual drug addict or alcoholic. The usual response is acknowledging that there may be a problem, but it's not a big deal, or it's not that bad. Others may persuade themselves, through denial and self-deception, that they can stop drinking when they want to, or that *"I still have a job or I am still married, or I am still paying my mortgage, and I don't sleep under a bridge, or I don't eat from the garbage can, real alcoholics and addicts are homeless. I am not any of these things. Therefore, I am not an alcoholic nor a drug addict."*

Drinkers who consider themselves functioning alcoholics believe that there is no serious problem that warrants taking urgent and drastic action. This misguided thinking gives the justification to continue the abusive and poisonous relationship with alcohol and drugs, with serious long-term consequences to the drinker and his family. AA meeting rooms are full of so-called functional alcoholics who fell from the ivory towers of success while drinking 'harmless' alcohol. Alcoholism may not always present itself as harmful but remember that it is a cunning and progressive disease.

Successful recovery requires you to develop a clear, accurate, and correct understanding of the problem of alcohol and drug addiction. This can be accomplished by asking and answering two simple but critical questions. The first question is: **Do I have a Problem?** If the answer is yes, you proceed to the second: **What is the problem?** If you answer "No" to the first question, then you may have no business to be on recovery therapy because you have nothing from which to recover. Some people in recovery programs don't believe they have a problem, and all they do is complain and sleep instead of paying attention and condemn any program if it doesn't work. Such people forget recovery programs work for those who need help because they believe they have a problem they have failed to solve independently.

Do I Have a Problem with Alcohol?

The above question looks simple and rather obvious. However, a closer look at the behavior of an alcoholic and drug addict reveals it resembles the life of someone who has lived in the mud for so long that being in the mud feels just as comfortable as being at home. Turning sides and changing your position in the mud brings no relief to your plight. The mud is mud, no matter how you look at it. Alcoholism and drug addiction are cases where you are both the victim and the perpetrator. No one visits it upon you except yourself. Therefore, answering the above question honestly and accurately is essential to successful recovery because many alcoholics and drug addicts continue using the harmful substances even when such behavior creates problems in health, family, financial, legal, work, educational, and marriage issues. Today, the alcoholic drinks; wakes up tomorrow feeling sick, sweaty, hung-over, miserable, and swears that *"I will never do this again."* However, at the end of the day, if not earlier, the alcoholic is back to drinking again. This begs the question: Why does a person continue drinking alcohol and doing drugs despite accumulating problems or even when it is unsafe to do so? Identifying and clarifying the problem helps in coming up with the correct solution. You cannot solve a problem that you cannot describe accurately. You cannot solve a problem you believe you don't have. You cannot solve a problem whose existence you deny.

You may know what to do to stop alcohol and drugs and stay sober, but you don't do it. Not doing what you are supposed to do is not because you are weak or not smart. You continue drinking and abuse drugs because you are not convinced that a problem exists. Sometimes you are convinced but lack the willingness and motivation to stop. Your actions demonstrate being convinced and not just what you say. When you become convinced, your actions will match your words. Alcoholics and drug addicts declare they know they have a problem, but they do nothing to relieve the problem. Knowing a problem and keeping on wallowing in it is just as good as being ignorant of that problem. Knowledge is power, but only if you use the knowledge.

A common tendency is not seeing the addiction problem as a problem but as something else, such as saying, *"This is the way I grew up. I have been drinking since I was a kid. This is my way of life, and I see nothing wrong."* You may admit to having a problem but still cannot pinpoint precisely what is wrong and what needs fixing. What usually happens is focusing on the symptoms instead of going to the heart of the problem. When asked, "What is your problem?" addicts seeking help often respond:

"Alcohol is the problem, drinking too much."

"My life, my mind, I am the problem."

"My wife, if she could stop the yelling and screaming."

"My husband, if only he can accept me as I am."
"Sleeping is the problem."

"My job, too much stress."

"My supervisor, he is a slave-master, and he doesn't care."

"My family members are too nosy. They should leave me alone and mind their own business."

"Body pain from the automobile accident is the problem."

"I have PTSD."

"If the depression and anxiety could go away, I wouldn't have to drink so much."

"I lost my dog, or some loved one, and that is why I drink so much."

The above is a list of what looks like the problem. In reality, these are symptoms and not the problem. I shall explore later more about the symptoms of the addiction problem in the book.

Lack of understanding and clarity of alcoholism and drug addiction makes the alcohol/drug user's life look like a continuous downhill journey that goes on precariously and with no end in sight. It is like a cargo train moving down the slope, out of gear and without brakes, and therefore the driver does not understand how to stop the train and wonders if there will be another crash today. Sometimes the downhill slide is broken when the alcoholic passes out, blacks out, gets arrested for DUI, or the money runs out.

Below are examples of patterns of drinking, followed by problems, drinking more, and getting into more problems:

Gomba: *"When I drank wine, I couldn't walk and often got seriously injured from never-ending falls. I would hurt myself and could not go to work. However, I would drink again, even when the injuries were still fresh, and I had broken ribs. I would also yell and scream at my daughters and then drink some more to cover up the guilt and shame. It was a miserable life to drink daily, isolate, and push away the people I love and care for so much."* The question is, why didn't Gomba stop drinking despite these conspicuous problems directly associated with alcohol consumption?

Booster: *"There came a time when I needed a shot to get out of bed and go to work in the morning. At first, I was adding some Vodka into my coffee and sip it on the way, and that would keep me calm until mid-morning when the jitters and shaking started. I couldn't bring the alcohol into the workplace because there is security everywhere. So, I devised a plan to bring a bottle, which I kept in the car. I would dash to the car during the break to have my fix. I kept toothpaste, mouth wash, chewing gum, and perfume in the car to use as soon as I finished getting my fix. I was unsafe driving while drinking and I risked losing my job, but I didn't care then. My alcohol was more important than my job and life. I didn't see any problem with that. Sometimes, I would call off sick because of hangovers and throbbing headaches. I got a wake-up call when I was arrested for DUI, stayed in jail for three days, and walked into the courtroom in shackles."* Again, the question is, why didn't Booster stop drinking despite these conspicuous problems directly associated with alcohol consumption?

Three factors that prompt change are choice, imposition, and crisis. You can change before things get out of hand or wait for change to be imposed on you by an employer, spouse, or other family members. The alcoholic rarely does well under the first two factors and keeps on drinking until a crisis happens. Alcoholics and drug addicts experience frequent problems but take no action to change until they have reached the bottom of the bottom. Why doesn't the drinker take action earlier to stop the fall? When does a problem become a serious one that warrants decisive corrective action by the drinker and drug addict?

The experiences presented above raise questions such as How many years have you been using alcohol and drugs while experiencing such behavior problems? What were your good reasons for continuing to drink and abuse drugs when it caused you such problems? How wise is your habit of continuing to drink and abuse drugs when that created frequent problems for you? Since when did it become okay to fall in the same ditch again and again? How much longer are you willing to continue drinking and experiencing the same troubles? How much time and money do you still want to invest in alcohol and drugs?

Alcohol abuse and drug addiction are disorders that work best through self-diagnosis. No one can persuade and convince you have a problem with alcohol or drugs except yourself. Your parents, friends, spouse, and anyone else will fail in making you quit drinking. Some people may have been telling you that you have a problem, but their words fell on deaf ears. Self-examination, accompanied by honesty and detailed responses to the above questions, should assist you in answering the question, "Do I have a problem?"

Here is Bregga's story:

Bregga is a 32-year-old male who started smoking marijuana at 14 years of age. Before marijuana, his school grades were excellent, and he was well-behaved at home and outside. He was well-liked by his friends and teachers. Six months of smoking weed saw a sharp rise in disciplinary problems at school and arguments at home with his parents. His grades deteriorated until he dropped out of high school. He went deep into drug dealing and pushing, which saw him arrested many times. Each time he returned from jail, he promised to stay sober, but nothing changed. He couldn't hold on to a job. He was often evicted from apartments for unruly behavior and non-payment of rent. He became a misfit among his people and unwelcome at family gatherings. He violently argued with anyone who talked about his drug habit and told him to seek help. He told his loved ones that he didn't need any help because he did not have a problem. He accused family members of being the ones with problems and needing help, and not himself. Bregga kept promising that things would get better, but his life became more reckless, violent, disorderly, and was often homeless.

There are many people out there who are like Bregga. It buries them in alcohol and drug abuse problems, but they vow that there is nothing wrong with that lifestyle.

Signs and Symptoms of Your Problem with Alcohol

Few people understand the disease of alcohol and drug addiction, but everyone is quick to offer solutions that don't work because they don't address the real problem. Most of the advice given to addicts and efforts taken are often directed at symptoms while the problem persists. Symptoms are just that, symptoms. They are not the problem. They show the existence of a problem. Recognizing and identifying symptoms should lead you to the underlying problem. Alcohol and drug abuse is the common factor associated with each of the problems you encountered during your drinking years, especially the repetitive ones in your health, finances, relationships, and work. Unfortunately, you devoted a lot of time and effort trying to deal with the symptoms, only to find that your drinking and drug abuse were getting worse even after the symptoms cleared. Dealing with symptoms does not eliminate the problem. Some people ended their marriages because they thought divorce was the solution. Unfortunately, the addiction problem did not go away. Others moved to new cities because they were convinced that their current living environment was the problem, only to discover that more alcohol and drugs were waiting for them in the new city.

Dwelling on the symptoms is misleading and often makes you think you don't have a problem with alcohol and drugs. Symptoms may blind you from seeing and understanding that the problem is drinking alcohol and not the body pain or lack of sleep. Focusing too much on the symptoms leaves the problem unattended to and intact. You cannot solve a problem by treating its symptoms only.

There are many clear indicators of problems directly linked to alcohol consumption and drug abuse. There are many red flags along the road to becoming an alcoholic and drug addict. You often ignore these danger warning signs on your way to the bottom. A pattern develops whereby you get drunk or become high today, run into problems today, go back to using the intoxicating stuff the following day, and the next day you face more problems. All this time, you ignore the red flags shouting, "Stop! Stop! Stop! Deadly bottomless pit ahead!"

Even if the symptoms seem obvious, you continue taking alcohol and using drugs day after day, thinking that today will be different and that you will be able to drink and take drugs normally and safely. Below is a list of some symptoms of the disease alcoholism and drug addiction:

1. Always being exhausted.
2. Being upset when not drinking or doing drugs.
3. Failing to stop using drugs and drinking when desiring to do so.
4. Pre-occupation with alcohol and drugs and therefore being unhappy about work, career, or life.
5. Bank account is always being overdrawn to support the substance abuse habit. Most times, the bank account is nonexistent.
6. Not accepting criticism when wrong. Engaging in denial, being argumentative, defensive, and engaging in lying habit.
7. Abandoning hobbies and other interests in favor of alcohol and drugs.
8. Staying in unhappy and unfulfilling relationships that are sometimes unsafe, abusive, and violent.
9. Believing you are responsible for, and feel guilty about, the death of a loved one because you were always too drunk and high to visit them during their last days.
10. Being always in Pawn Shops, getting rid of valuable family possessions.
11. Being always in the streets, hustling, looking for cash.
12. Being dishonest to self, family, friends, and anyone else.

13. Working hard a lot (sometimes 2 to 3 jobs) but there is nothing to show for the hard work: accomplishing not much, if anything, because of alcohol and drugs.

14. Being selfish and over-controlling your loved ones.

15. Stopping going to church and having no more prayers.

16. Being offended at inappropriate times and situations.

17. Convincing yourself that alcohol is good for sleep but often with contrary results.

18. Drinking and driving — with no recollection of how you got home, then looking for the car the next day.

19. Reducing interactions with loved ones — isolating, ignoring them, and pushing them away so they can leave you alone to enjoy alcohol and drugs.

20. Drinking first thing in the morning.

21. Drinking at work, you believe you can stop after a few drinks.

22. Spending money on alcohol and drugs before paying bills.

23. Believing it won't be bad this time (gets worse anyway).

24. Ignoring concerns or complaints raised by loved ones (Believing that after all of your drinking that it is not that bad).

25. Thinking that everyone is against you. Blaming them for ganging up against you, the 'innocent' victim.

26. Having a-despairing and defeated attitude wherever you are. Believing that nothing ever works, feeling helpless, hopeless, and having self-pity. You are using alcohol to treat feelings.

27. Trying to limit yourself or self-control while drinking.

28. Hiding drinking to minimize the quantity and frequency of drinking.

28. Deceiving self that you drink normally, like others, unaware that you are an abnormal drinker.

The above list is not exhaustive. It covers some warning signs indicating a problem with alcohol and drugs. Unfortunately, these signs will be ignored through denial, justification, rationalization, and lame excuses, which give you the urge to continue using.

What Is the Problem? Stop Focusing on the Symptoms

Assuming that you are now convinced that you have a problem, the next step is to find out exactly what the problem is. Alcoholics and drug addicts often come to a point where they speak, *"I have reached the bottom. I have lost everything in my life. There is nothing left. I am done. I am sick and tired of being sick and tired. I have tried everything, and nothing works. I don't know what to do."* When asked to identify the problem, such people state: *The problem is me, the drinking, the alcohol, the cocaine, the heroin, the denying, or being too proud to cry out for help.* Others display a lack of understanding of the problem and attribute it to drinking too much, limiting the number of drinks, drinking alone at home, drinking first thing in the morning, having too much alcohol in the fridge at home, or switching from whisky to wine. These erroneous assumptions are lame excuses that show a complete lack of understanding of the problem.

To the alcoholic, it looks like his/her problem is drinking too much or never drinking in the morning or any of the list of signs and symptoms stated above. Behaviors such as limiting the number of drinks and vowing never to drink during business hours are symptoms of the larger problem of alcoholism, which is powerlessness. Trying to moderate drinking does not solve the problem, so is the decision to never drink during business hours. Signs and symptoms are not the problem. They show the existence of a problem. Symptoms are the loudest evidence of the presence of the problem, although the alcoholic and drug addict may think that all is well. Signs and symptoms point to the existence of the disease of alcoholism. Excuses, justification, and pretense show ignorance of the problem, and that is why the alcoholic continues to drink even if it's causing him a lot of trouble.

Vague and inaccurate understanding of the problem leads to challenges in recovery that are accompanied by frequent relapses. Denial and giving the problem other names does not make it go away. There is no right way of doing the wrong thing. Lack of understanding of the problem triggers wrong solutions and fruitless recovery efforts, which keep you stuck in the vicious addiction cycle instead of moving you to a new life of sobriety and freedom. Poor understanding of the diseases of alcoholism and drug addiction causes relapses accompanied by hopelessness and helplessness. Many alcoholics and drug addicts are in and out of treatment programs and have no clue how to overcome the addiction. Others have attended ninety AA/NA meetings in ninety days and still relapse. No amount of hard work, determination, and energy will help to solve a poorly and inaccurately identified problem.

The Phenomenon of Craving

In order to get a clear and accurate picture of the diseases of alcoholism and drug addiction, we must remove the mask of excuses, denial, and justification. It does not hide the problem. You don't have to go far to see the problem unfolding and in real-time. It is in plain sight and always announces itself every time you take the first drink. Watch, observe, and look at your behavior pattern immediately after taking the very first drink of the day. The first drink is the key to understanding the disease of alcoholism. The first drink always triggers the physical desire for subsequent drinks. You use your rational mind to take the first drink. After the first drink, rational choice is slowly replaced by the physical body's unquenched thirst for another one and yet another. Each drink you take increases the physical urges for more. As the number of drinks increases, your rational mind gets more and more intoxicated and impaired by alcohol. More drinks continue to impair your judgment while increasing bodily physical cravings for more alcohol. After the first few drinks, the body takes over because now the mind is too intoxicated and relaxed to think rationally and realistically. When normal thinking stops, you make illogical choices dictated by the urgent and often irresistible need of the body for more alcohol.

Once the body takes over the driver's seat, you are now free to drink until you pass out because the mind is no longer in control; it is sleeping on duty. You are now free to drink more than you intended because your body demands more of the liquid. Your thinking, rational mind, your voice of reason has lost its ability to help you stop. If you drink water, tea, coffee, or soda, your mind and body will let you know when to stop. This is no longer possible after several alcoholic drinks because the mind is now incapable and incapacitated through intoxication. One or two drinks are never enough. The alcoholic never gets enough because of the cravings triggered by the first drink. The first drink is the culprit because the physical urges do not occur if you don't take it. Sometimes you drank until you pass out, although your original intention was to have a few. Passing out was not in your plan when you started drinking that day. Being arrested for DUI was never in your plan when you left home to go out for a drink. You completely expected to return home and not to sleep in jail.

Normal vs. Abnormal Drinkers

There are two types of alcohol users, normal and abnormal drinker. The difference can be detected by observing what happens after the first drink. Abnormal alcohol users testify to their inability to stop once they take the first drink. This inability to stop is also true about drugs after taking the first pill, smoking the first joint, or snorting the first line. Normal alcohol drinkers can stop after one or two drinks. Some normal drinkers may take hours with one drink or may not even finish the first drink and leave it at the table. Abnormal drinkers may not understand the wisdom of people who leave alcohol at the counter. They think it's such a waste of money and a valuable asset. Normal drinkers can stop because they begin to feel dizzy, sick, nauseous, and out of control after a drink or two, making it uncomfortable to keep drinking.

On the other hand, the first drink triggers the phenomenon of craving, which makes the abnormal drinker want more and more alcohol. Abnormal drinkers are allergic to alcohol. This may sound counterintuitive but recall that alcohol is a toxic substance with no nutritional value. The human body is supposed to reject any toxic substance, but this does not happen with abnormal drinkers. A normal drinker can stop after the first one because his body rejects more of the poison. Instead of rejecting alcohol, the body of the alcoholic relaxes and feels mellow after the first few drinks, prompting cravings for more.

Unknown to the abnormal drinker is that the more you drink, the more the craving and, therefore, the more drinks needed to quench the craving. When you are drinking, judgment is the first aspect impaired by alcohol, followed by other senses such as vision, hearing, memory, and motor skills. After the 1st, 2nd, or 3rd drink, the body takes over control of the decision-making responsibility. When the mind is no longer functioning, the body gives the instructions and tells you to order more drinks, even if you are already very drunk.

Human behavior naturally arises from the mind and should ideally be stopped by the mind. This is not the case for the abnormal alcohol user because, at some point, the body takes over the crucial task of thinking and choosing. The body does not know when to stop, and the mind is too drunk to think in ordinary ways. The cravings for more are in the body and not in your mind, and it is difficult to stop drinking once the cravings kick in. So you end up drinking more than initially intended. The craving phenomenon, aroused by the first drink, helps explain why people drink until they pass out or why a person still wants more alcohol even after consuming large quantities of the stuff or drinks until the early hours of the morning.

Consumption of unintended large volumes of alcohol or drugs is often followed by morning sickness, headaches, pitiful regrets, hangover, sullen and weak rhetorical questions like *"Why did I do this to myself?"* and a firm declaration that *"I will never do this again."* While drinking and abusing drugs, you may remember prior commitments such as waking up early for work, attending family gatherings or being present at your children's school events or birthday. After a few drinks, you may say to yourself, *"It's time to stop and go home so that I can wake up early for work or be home before the kids go to sleep or attend a special family anniversary."* This decision to stop and go home is often immediately followed by another decision to drink one for the road, another, and another and another until we abandon these other obligations.

When morning comes, a realization of loss of control over alcohol and memory loss of details on the previous night's events may give rise to self-pity, despair, and resignation. The negative after-effects of alcohol and drugs force the user to declare once more, *"I don't know why I am drinking so much. I want to stop, and I will never do this again."* Unfortunately, this unhappy pattern is repeated and again as you plunge headlong to the bottom of the bottom. Any of the three options become very viable, which are jail, hospital, or death.

Mental Obsession

During your drug abuse and drinking career, there came a time when you got sick and tired of being sick and tired. Your inability to control alcohol, drugs, and other important aspects of your life may have forced you to quit. You became sober for a period ranging from a few days, weeks, months to years. Initially, you were excited to be sober. There was a victory at last, and you started getting your life back together.

The thrill and excitement are often short-lived, as you soon discover that sober life can be dull and not so joyful. Continue living your life even when you sober up. However, the fun, the excitement, the Thank God It's Friday (TGIF), and the Happy Hour are no longer there. Life, being life, always comes with challenges that make you feel restless, discontented, irritable, frustrated, and other related negative emotions. As these uncomfortable and unhappy experiences and emotions persist, your alcoholic and drug-addicted memory remembers the sense of ease and comfort that comes with the first drink or first joint. You may fight and resist the temptation to drink because you decided to quit. Now a tug of war ensues inside you, with one side saying, *"Drink and feel better,"* while the opposing side says, *"Remember, you decided to quit and stay sober."* You might have even promised your loved ones that you want to change and be sober. You may block the urge to drink to honor your promise to yourself and your loved ones, but the boredom and misery get stronger and more intense.

Each day of frustration and unhappiness intensifies the mental obsession, causing the desire to drink to get stronger and out of control. As the obsession rises, you become preoccupied with a great need for relief from the feelings of unhappiness, loneliness, boredom, and general discomfort. The obsession weakens and erodes your resolve to stay sober when life seems to be dull and no fun. The intensified mental obsession will ultimately force you to break your promise to stay sober.

Admit the Problem: What is to Admit?

After you have successfully examined and answered the two questions, *"Do I have a problem?"* and *"What is the Problem?"* the next important step is to admit the problem. The first step from Alcoholic Anonymous states that *"We admitted we were powerless over alcohol and that our lives had become unmanageable."*

Narcotics Anonymous version states the first step, *"We admitted we were powerless over our addiction, that our lives had become unmanageable."* Taking this first step and admitting that you have a drinking and drug abuse problem can be difficult and scary, but it is the foundation of all positive change.

Such admission is critically important for alcohol and drug addicts because they have had the problem of powerlessness for many years while oblivious to its existence and presence in your life. Admitting powerlessness is the real beginning of the recovery process. The healing starts here; you cannot go any further in sobriety until you have admitted you have the problem. It is not enough to feel your way through recovery by intuition or guesswork. It is, therefore, imperative to understand what you are doing when you admit. What is to admit?

There are various ways to describe what it is to admit, and these include:

1. To acknowledge.
2. To truly believe you have a problem (not fake news anymore).
3. To surrender.
4. To own up and stop blaming.
5. To take responsibility and accountability for your behaviors and actions.
6. To accept and embrace the truth that you were wrong all these years in believing that alcohol and drugs were your good friends.

To admit is to accept the reality that alcohol and drugs were not your friends and will never be. It is genuinely acknowledging that you have been delusional most of your drinking and drug abuse days. Admitting allows the reality to sink in that you have been an abnormal drinker all these years, never normal, and will remain abnormal unless you abstain. When you admit, you are opening yourself to the reality that you were insane, your drinking and drug use patterns were insanity, your motives to drink and do drugs were driven by insanity, and that your beliefs about alcohol and drugs were insane too. To admit is accepting that you pretended you were okay all along, all was well, nothing was wrong when in fact everything was wrong. It is seeing the truth that sets you free, which is that the so-called nice times bankrupted your integrity, your dignity, and your relationships with yourself and your loved ones.

To admit is to face the truth that you were lying to yourself all these years and saw nothing wrong with it. Many alcoholics and drug addicts swear that they never lied to anyone and were always upfront and honest about their alcohol and drug use. You may not have lied openly to the outside world, but you lied to yourself when you said, *"I can quit anytime." "I can have a few and stop." "My marriage is the problem and not me."* All these were lies to yourself, and you have to admit the self-deception and the dishonesty to yourself and other people you harmed by your addiction lifestyle.

Admit the Problem is Powerlessness over Alcohol and Not Something Else

When you have abstained, any resistance to drinking and drug abuse is weakened by the mental obsession. You still want to be sober, but the obsession is overwhelming and consuming. As you resolve to stay sober, the obsession

43

progressively gets stronger and intense; the place, day, and time will come when you give up the fight and reach out for the first drink or first opiate pill. Now you are back to square one. When you relapse, your first drink will trigger the craving, which causes physical bodily urges for more alcohol to quench it. You have rushed back to the vicious cycle where you want to stop but cannot due to the phenomenon of craving. You want to quit but cannot due to mental obsession. The combination of **bodily craving** and **mental obsession** are the factors that make you powerless over alcohol. Most alcoholics and drug addicts are not fully persuaded that they have a problem with alcohol and drugs, let alone aware that they are powerless over alcohol and drugs. Some may sing the chorus of being powerless over alcohol but do not understand how they are powerless because they drink like any other person in the bar. Many others continue drinking wrongly believing that they have no problem, stop when they want to, or that everything is under control.

We can sum the disease of alcohol up in this way:

> *You want to stop, but you cannot because of the craving in the body triggered by the first drink.*

> *You want to quit, but you cannot because of mental obsession.*

The conclusion is that you are powerless over alcohol because of the craving and the mental obsession.

CHAPTER THREE

More About the Problem: Consequences of Powerlessness

A major consequence of powerlessness is that the life of the alcoholic and drug addict increasingly becomes unmanageable. Management is about getting the desired results. The difference between good and bad management lies in the results. Life is unmanageable when you no longer experience desired outcomes in essential areas of your life. The undesirable consequences of alcoholism are proof that you are powerless and that your life has become unmanageable. The signs of unwanted results include passing out while drinking, inability to recall what happened the previous night, frequent arguments with loved ones, strife involving friends and family, internal conflict, and lack of inner peace about the deteriorating drinking patterns.

Other experiences that may go on the list include health issues exacerbated by alcoholism, problems at work, at home, and at school, financial and legal issues, problems with the law linked to alcohol and drug abuse, and patterns of numbing painful emotions emanating from alcohol and drugs. Another important aspect of life negatively affected by alcohol and drug consumption is relationships. Start by examining the relationship you had with yourself while drinking, then move to relationships with other people such as family, friends, co-workers, and neighbors.

Below are some real-life examples of how alcohol makes different aspects of life unmanageable, starting with health: In what specific ways was your health unmanageable because of powerlessness over alcohol and drugs?

As an aspect of your life, we divide your health into three components: physical, mental, and spiritual health.

Your Physical Health

In what specific ways was your "Physical Health" unmanageable because of powerlessness over alcohol and drugs? The ways include:

- Feeling sick and bad, but you don't care—no eating or sleeping for many days.

- Getting anxious and sick while waiting for a dealer to deliver heroin. Stomach cramps, getting sweaty, chills, but you remain undeterred because heroin is your medicine. Even the nauseating sickness is not a problem because your fix is on the way.

- Hands are shaking, dry heaving, feeling sick like hell, being dehydrated, not drinking any water, etc.

- Being malnourished from drinking too much alcohol on an empty stomach.

- Many visits to emergency rooms for alcohol-drug related ailments -bruises, cuts, gunshot wounds, drug overdose, high blood pressure, fatty liver, withdrawal pains, road accident injuries, etc.

- Falling while drunk or high, broken bones.

- Staggering around with slurred speech.

- Drinking till you get sick, drinking some more the next day to feel better, or just spending the whole day sleeping hopelessly and helplessly, only waking up to go to the bathroom.

- Serious health problems, but you continue using drugs and drinking without caring—frequent hospitalizations.

- Gaining weight, you had worked so hard to lose; face looking puffy, swollen, and unattractive.

Your Mental Health

In what specific ways was your "Mental Health" unmanageable because of powerlessness over alcohol and drugs? These ways may include the following:

1. Extreme personality changes.

2. Feeling isolated, always unhappy, anxious, sad, depressed, suicidal, and homicidal.

3. Being always worried and fearful that something terrible is going to happen.

4. Being always quick to descend into anger, rage, irritation, restlessness, discontent, and agitation.

5. Feeling bad, guilty, shameful, scared, and insecure; drinking some more alcohol to numb these feelings.

6. Feeling helpless and hopeless; inability to control or stop drinking and using drugs.

7. Feeling empty inside, with no inner peace, no inner strength.

8. Rapid mood swings, agitated and impatient with kids, spouse; screaming and shouting at them, and blaming them for your troubles.

9. Starting to drink early in the morning, drinking daily, drinking during work hours, and continuing to drink after work until early morning hours.

10. Being physically and mentally ill from drugs—headaches, running nose, painful throat and teeth, body aches, feeling hot and sweaty, afraid to go to the doctor, missing scheduled appointments,

fearing being caught. You are losing your will to do anything positive and being helpless and hopeless.

11. Forgetfulness, memory lapse, talking on the phone for long periods but not remembering conversations and the plans agreed on during the talks; Struggling to put the pieces together.

12. Drinking so as not to worry or not to care about what is going on. However, ending up increasing the frequency and intensity of worrying, especially the day after.

13. Not believing what people say you did the night before. Having no memory of the things after you drank over the edge.

Your Spiritual Health

In what specific ways was your "Spiritual Health" unmanageable because of powerlessness over alcohol and drugs? These may include:

- Quitting praying or reading the bible and only praying when in a fix, for help to get out of trouble.

- Feeling bad, guilty, shame, and fear that you are beyond rescue, and God will not forgive you.

- Beating yourself up for the inability to control your drinking and drug abuse, criticizing yourself and judging yourself harshly, pulling yourself down by drinking more and more, believing you are beyond help.

- Feeling spiritually and emotionally bankrupt, barren, and harsh lifestyle. Nothing works for you anymore.

- Now, your total trust shifts from God to alcohol. You come to depend on alcohol, rely on alcohol, and have your confidence in alcohol. If you want to celebrate, you go to alcohol. If you are going through bad times, alcohol is your buddy.

- Being angry with God for the troubles you are going through, blaming Him for your suffering from alcohol and drugs, accusing Him of letting you down, for not saving your marriage or your job, or for some other loss you experienced while using alcohol and drugs.

- Doubting the existence of God, fearing that God cannot help you anymore, therefore relying on alcohol, trusting in alcohol, having faith and confidence in alcohol and drugs.

Your Financial Life

In what specific ways was your "Financial Life" unmanageable because of powerlessness over alcohol and drugs? The following could be some ways:

- Always running out of money for essentials, all money went to drugs or alcohol.

- Buying cheap junky food or going without food.

- Bills and credit cards go unpaid.

- Alcohol and drugs become more important than paying bills and buying food. Destroying credit record because of huge unpaid debts and living in constant fear of the creditors.

- Spending a lot of money that one does not have and being persistently hounded by creditors and debt collectors.

- Having regular power cuts, an empty refrigerator, an empty stomach, and an empty life.

- Making up stories, lying to get money.

- Working very hard to earn money and quickly hand it to the drug dealer and liquor store, having nothing to show for it except regrets, self-pity, self-trashing, misery, and despair.

- Pawning valuable possessions and telling lies to cover up.

- Not working due to alcohol and drug abuse. Any money scrapped together supports the addiction.

- Having no ambition to undertake worthwhile or life-changing projects, no drive for success, no motivation to achieve anything significant, and comfortable doing the bare minimum.

- Being always worried about lack of money and mounting debts; being fearful for no hope of getting the money next.

- Making huge and high-value financial investments while high or intoxicated.

- Losing money repeatedly to gambling, drugs, alcohol, prostitution, and doing nothing to change this persistently dysfunctional pattern, doing it again and again after each loss, hoping that it would be different and better this time. Unfortunately, financial losses are getting worse and never better.

- Indulging in shopping sprees as a cure for self-loathing, anger, rejection, and frustration.

-

- Feeling shameful about not being able to take care of yourself financially and having no courage to ask for help, resorting to stealing, cheating, lying to loved ones, and making flimsy excuses to get money to support the addiction beast.

Relationship with Yourself

What was the quality of the relationship you had with yourself when you were drinking alcohol? How much quality time did you spend with yourself? Describe your "me time," which is the quality time you had with yourself when abusing drugs and alcohol. In what specific ways was your "Relationship with Yourself" unmanageable because of powerlessness over alcohol and drugs? Here are some common ways:

- Not caring about looks, hygiene, and neglecting showers and grooming.

- Having low self-respect and low self-esteem. Not loving self anymore. Considering yourself valueless, worthless.

- Having a fragile future focus, having dim or no prospects, being stagnant, stuck in life. It preoccupies you with obtaining the next drink and how to get through the day.

- Tolerating discomfort and inconvenience.

- Hating self, feeling like a loser, a chronic failure.

- Lack of inhibition — going out with anyone and feeling disgusted the following morning.

- Dishonesty to self and others.

- Loss of clear personal identity, not knowing who you are anymore, and being unhappy with what you have become.

- No longer experiencing normal feelings; if they show up, you suppress them fast with alcohol and drugs. Self-medicating.

- Feeling so messed up, you think your loved ones would be better off without you.

- Fearing that you might die young from perpetual self-destruction caused by alcohol and drugs.

- Feeling you are getting old, not knowing where you are going with your life, having nothing to show for your old age.

- Considering yourself to be a social drinker or functioning alcoholic but continuing to over-drink, with serious consequences.

- Neglecting basic house chores: dishes pile up, laundry piles up, the house is extremely messy. All visitors are no longer welcome to your house.

Relationship with Your Family and Friends

What kind of relationship did you have with your family and friends when you were abusing drugs and alcohol? How much love, trust, and respect were there between you and your family members? In what specific ways was your "Relationship with Your Family and Friends" unmanageable because of powerlessness over alcohol and drugs? These ways are, but not limited to:

- Not being a good husband/wife, brother/sister, or neighbor. It seems like nothing you do goes right.

- Ignoring and violating the interests and rights of loved ones.

- Taking friendships for granted.

- Isolating and pushing loved one's away while proclaiming you love them dearly.

- Failure understanding conversations with family or friends, only talking to them when high or drunk, and not recalling conversations the following day.

- Getting good at being lazy, lying, impatient, irritable, flippant, and intolerant of others; it's all about you.

- Manipulating, exploiting, using, and abusing friends and family, taking advantage of others.

- Extreme carelessness; letting others take advantage of you.

- Being physically, vocally, and mentally abusive; forcing your will on harmless loved ones, your innocent victims. Intentionally and deliberately hurting and belittling others.

- Mom, dad, spouse, and your kids are constantly worried and are scared that you will die and leave them.

- Losing the trust and respect of kids, parents, and friends.

- Losing your trust and respect for yourself.

- Cutting out family and friends for complaining about your drinking and drug abuse.

- Saying hurtful things to other people and claiming that you are telling the truth.

- Using anger and threats to silence people into submission to get what you want and sometimes to get relief from the pain inside.

Your Marriage(s)

What was the quality of your marriage(s) when you were drinking alcohol? How much love, trust, respect, and affection were there? If you are single, don't feel exempted from examining and answering these questions. Instead of marriage, focus on the romantic relationships you had while drinking alcohol. In what specific ways was your "Marriage Relationship" unmanageable because of powerlessness over alcohol and drugs? The ways could include those listed below:

- Spouse no longer trusts you. Having no respect for and no intimacy with a spouse and hurting a spouse significantly because of your alcohol and drug abuse -- always arguing, fighting, and frequently calling the police.

- Spouse always being worried about you and being disappointed by your endless lies about where you were, with whom, and what you were doing.

- Kids always being disappointed, angry, and hurting from seeing you passed out, missing their important functions for no valid reason, and embarrassing them in front of their friends.

- Going through a divorce, battling for kids, setting up private investigators on each other to come up with evidence that the other spouse is the bad one, not a suitable parent.

- Wondering and being fearful about "Will we stay together," that spouse might threaten to leave you any day or has.

- Being envious of a happy close relationship between kids and your spouse while you shy away from them, isolating, pushing them away, concentrating on your alcohol and drugs.

- Promising spouse to quit but continuing to sneak drinks into the home, getting caught again, forgiven again, attending AA to silence spouse, then giving up after a few meetings accompanied by weak attempts to stay sober. Complaining AA does not work for you, it's for alcoholics, and you are not one of them. Continuing to drink, being given a spouse's final warning to either quit abusing alcohol or leave. You don't know what to do. Maybe seeking treatment, which you hate so much and therefore discharging yourself before completing the program.

- Being too high, too drunk, or too tired to spend time with spouse and kids.

Lost Love, Respect, and Trust

You lost the love, respect, and trust of your loved ones while drinking and doing drugs. Can you list some specific things you did to lose their love, respect, and trust? These could include:

- Parading their flaws while ignoring your own deplorable habits and behaviors.

- Stopping calling them and answering their calls, cutting them off from your world.

- Not being on time for special family events.

- Son/daughter pleading with you and begging you to stop alcohol/drugs and pretending to listen, even making promises which you quickly forget and continue taking alcohol—ignoring the wonderful and innocent people in your life because it's all about you.

- Not valuing your loved one's feelings and concerns about using drugs and alcohol, paying lip service, and nothing more.

- Lying about your using alcohol and drugs, manipulating loved ones for money, making them look like they are the reason for your drinking.

- Staying out drinking and not going to bed with a spouse.

- Stealing money and pain pills from spouse, parents, grandparents, etc.

- Spending little time with aging parents and hurting them badly.

- Being stubborn, rebellious, difficult, impossible to deal with, resistant, overly sarcastic, and making fun out of serious matters.

- Missing from home and loved ones for long periods and not wanting them to know where you were and what you were doing.

- Experiencing near-death sickness, being hospitalized, being on the mend, discharged, and resuming drinking as nothing happened.

- Using money for rent, bills, and groceries to buy alcohol and drugs.

- Being physically present but emotionally and mentally distant, disconnected, and absent.

- Making alcohol and drugs more important than your career, spouse, and children.

- Being angry and jumping into a rage if your family finds out about your addiction habit.

- Over controlling family and unforgiving them for minor infractions or imagined wrongs, forgetting the ugly things you put them through.

- Borrowing a sibling's car, wrecking it while drunk, getting arrested for DUI, becoming angry with a sibling for not bailing you fast out of jail, arriving home, and continuing drinking in front of the sibling as if nothing happened.

- Having rapid mood swings, family members walking on eggshells as a result.

- Being mad and angry at your spouse for both enabling you and refusing to enable you. Either way, the spouse is always losing.

- Missing important planned family functions, lying that you are on the way but never showing up, others keep waiting for you.

- Cheating on spouse numerous times, sometimes spouse finding out and allowing you back into the relationship, continuing cheating without remorse.

- Spouse asking you to stop drinking, agreeing to stop but continuing to drink, anyway.

- Putting financial burden and other family pressures on spouse and then blaming the same helpful person for your endless troubles.

- Arriving very drunk at a family wedding, humiliating yourself, embarrassing your loved one in public, and then just shutting out, drunk.

- Using a sibling's house for partying with your buddies, leaving the house dirty and messed up for the sibling to clean it up.

- Drinking alcohol, blacking out, calling fire station claiming the house is on fire.

- Drinking and doing drugs, blacking out, having no memory of what you said or promised loved ones.

- Hurting loved one by not showing affection, not hugging them anymore.

Rebuilding Broken Relationships

Being sober is very important in your recovery work, but sobriety alone is not enough. There is a need to repair damaged relationships with the people in your life. You must work toward regaining the love and trust that you lost due to alcohol and a self-centered lifestyle. Saying *"I am sorry"* does not work anymore because you said it many times before. Making promises doesn't help because you made a lot of such empty promises while using alcohol. Expecting them to forgive you and embrace you quickly show a lack of sensitivity to the pain and suffering you made them endure. They didn't deserve the agony you put them through, and now you expect them to forget the past and welcome you as a hero in their lives. Rebuilding broken relationships requires your actions to speak louder than your words.

What specific things are you going to do to regain your loved ones' love, trust, and respect? The following are suggested:

- Do what you say you are going to do. Act on your word and deliver on your promises to your loved ones.

- Be open with your family about your recovery and keep them informed about your sobriety work.

- Be observant, paying attention to, and respecting their rights, interests, and welfare.

- Allow them to be where they are mentally, emotionally, and psychologically about you and your past addiction behavior.

- Take money and time to be with your aging mother, father, grandparents, etc. Take them out to eat.

- Hand over all that has to do with finances to your spouse.

- Spend quality time with your children and grandkids.

- Set boundaries for yourself and enforce them consistently and continuously.

- Stay mentally and physically active, pray daily and frequently, work with other addicts, give priority to your sobriety.

- Make new friends who are sober and responsible.

- Become honest, patient, tolerant, humble, and accepting.

- Get a job, become financially independent and responsible.

- Practice better time management by being punctual and showing up as expected.

- Go to bed with your spouse instead of staying downstairs, drinking some more alcohol.

Your Work/Job-Career Life

How did your alcohol use impact your work? What specific ways was your "Work/Job-Career" unmanageable because of powerlessness over alcohol and drugs? These include:

- Having inconsistently sloppy work habits, experiencing tardiness.

- Not being at work as expected.

- Calling in sick from work following a predictable pattern (e.g., Monday mornings or soon after payday).

- Neglecting work or just not paying attention. Being aware of your wrongdoing but doing it some more, anyway.

- Losing a string of jobs in a brief space of time, suffering demotions but not caring.

- Sleeping during the day at work, missing important meetings, procrastinating on assigned tasks, continually missing deadlines, and holding on to a job by a thread.

Your Legal Life

In what specific ways was your "Legal Life" unmanageable because of powerlessness over alcohol and drugs? Common such ways are:

- DUI arrests and jail time.

- Legal costs, huge lawyer's fees for DUI, court fees, heavy financial penalties all round.

- Long drawn-out, costly, emotionally draining, mentally, and physically exhausting divorce court battles.

- Court battles with creditors and debt collectors.

Your Transportation Status

In what specific ways was your "Transportation Status" unmanageable because of powerlessness over alcohol and drugs? You may have experienced:

- You have frequent road accidents, wrecked cars.

- Driving drunk and high most of the time is dangerous to self and others.

- Dozing off, sleeping on the wheel.

- Getting home but not recalling how you got there—wondering if your car is there outside the house, being surprised to see it.

- Cars getting repossessed for non-payment of car notes.
- Selling your car in exchange for drugs or to settle drug-related debts.

Your Housing Situation

In what specific ways was your "Housing Status" unmanageable because of powerlessness over alcohol and drugs? Listed below are common consequences:

- Non-payment of rent or mortgage.

- Losing your own home, becoming a destitute beggar living on the streets.

- Squatting with friends, being unwelcome at your parents' house, camping in your car.

- Being chased out of other people's homes for shameless over-drinking and sometimes stealing from your hosts.

- Being homeless, living in squalor, surviving on handouts and soup kitchens.
- Being unreliable, undependable, untrustworthy, and always on the move looking for the next place to call home, even if it's for one night.

- Tolerating suffering, becoming familiar with, and used to hardship, being friends with struggling, troubles, and lacking.

Your Hobbies

What hobbies did you engage in when you were doing alcohol?

How did you spend your spare time? How often did you go on vacation, and which vacation places did you visit? In what specific ways were your "Hobbies" unmanageable because of powerlessness over alcohol and drugs? The following are some effects of heavy drinking and abusing drugs:

- Give up hobbies and other healthy lifestyle interests.

- Having no motivation, no energy, no interest in things you used to enjoy.

- Losing membership to gym and health clubs.

- Alcohol and drugs are becoming the only form of recreation and no other valuable activities occupying your spare time and weekends.

- Pawning away sports gear, sports, and fishing equipment to raise money for alcohol and drugs.
- Manufacturing stories and lies to avoid joining others for physical exercises and healthy living activities.

- Stopping reading anything worthwhile and avoiding going to book clubs.

- Experiencing drastic change from being very outgoing and out-door oriented to someone who did not want to do anything. Isolating yourself and just lazing around at home.

Importance and Benefits of Admitting Powerlessness

Now that you are convinced that you have a problem and know for sure what the problem is and not just its symptoms, the next major step is to admit powerlessness. The self-analysis you have done so far should have persuaded you to admit that there is a real problem, not an imaginary one that needs your attention. You also admit that the problem of powerlessness has been there for a long time. To admit is to surrender finally, to have no more denial, no more pretense, no more blaming, no more excuses, and no more fabricated justifications.

To admit is to stop fighting the disease, stop resisting, give up, and give in. It is to accept that a problem exists which is more powerful than your limited five senses and, therefore, you cannot solve it by yourself without the aid of a greater power. To admit is to yield to the reality that you have failed; your efforts are not working, and that you need something greater and more powerful than yourself. Alcoholics who do self in recovery find it hard to stay sober. Admission is taking responsibility for your beliefs, choices, and actions. Admitting brings you to a position where you emphatically decide that you cannot continue the same way; you are coming up clean and opening up to the reality which has always been there.

To admit is to acknowledge the presence of a problem whose existence you denied for a long time. You are finally conceding to the fact that all along, you were a slave to alcohol; it has become your master, and it has taken control over your life. You practically demonstrate that you now know that you have not been in charge; alcohol was, and if you continue to drink, you will also continue to be a servant to alcohol. To admit is to surrender defeat, to throw in the towel.

What have you admitted? Some specific issues you are admitting are that you pushed away loved ones and let them down again, that you were dishonest to think that you were in control when in reality alcohol was, that you continued going in the wrong direction with both eyes open, that you knew something was wrong but did very little or nothing about it, that you were drinking and encountering problems but kept on drinking and deceiving yourself that it would get better, that you hurt yourself and others but remained convinced that your drinking harmed nobody.

You have admitted that alcohol and drugs were more important than paying bills, buying food, and spending quality time with family. You admit that you have a problem that you didn't know how to handle or do something about, that you were imprisoned and hospitalized by alcohol while walking around the streets, that you enjoyed being high but ignored the consequences, that you used anger to silence people and get what you wanted, that you forced your way through self-engineered predicaments sometimes to hide the pain inside.

The good news is that admitting powerlessness is the beginning of getting your power back. By admitting you are making the wise choice of deciding not to continue fighting a battle against alcohol and drugs that you are ever-losing. You are moving from delusional thinking and false hopes that things will get better to be in touch with the reality that you have been going in the wrong direction in a one-way street all these years. To admit is to tell yourself, and mean it, that you are no longer willing to invest your time and money in your downfall. You are commanding yourself to stop scoring own goals opposing yourself.

CHAPTER FOUR

The Solution: Power of Believing

You have so far established what the problem is, and now a solution is needed. The problem is powerlessness over alcohol. The consequences of powerlessness are that life becomes difficult, troubled, and full of hardships. Essential aspects of your life have been turned upside down. The solution to powerlessness is power, and nothing else will do. Any other solution will not give you the power necessary to abstain from alcohol. Moving to another city will not do it. Changing from whisky to wine will not do it either. Drinking after work or weekends only will not work.

What are Beliefs and from Where Do They Come?

Beliefs come from thoughts and feelings about any subject, issue, or topic. Suppose you keep thinking the same thoughts and experiencing the same feelings about a subject that produces a mood. The same mood over some time becomes an attitude. Your predominant daily thoughts, feelings, moods, and attitudes combine and become perceptions that become beliefs and habits. A belief is a thought which you keep on having. There are many sources of beliefs, such as upbringing, education, culture, reading materials, mass media.

What is Believing?

Believing is trusting in, relying on, depending on, and having confidence in something. Believing is a force that is always in operation. It doesn't matter whether you know it, whether you are aware of it, whether you like it or don't. Your beliefs can either work for you or against you. It doesn't matter whether you intend them to. You became powerless because you gave your power to alcohol. How so, you may ask? You believed in alcohol; you trusted in it; you relied on it; you depended on it, and you had confidence in it.

You believed so much in alcohol that you gave it your all and your best. As a result, you did whatever alcohol told you to do even when you opposed it. Sometimes you knew it was not appropriate to drink at that particular point, but you drank anyway because you no longer had the power to say no. How many times did you drink after you had vowed not to do it again?

Nature of Believing: Spiritual vs. Physical (Non-Spiritual)

There are sense knowledge-based believing, and that which is beyond the five senses. Beliefs based on senses are limited to what you can see, hear, feel, taste, and touch. Step 2 of the twelve steps of Alcoholic Anonymous describes the solution to powerlessness, *"Came to Believe That A Power Greater Than Ourselves Could Restore Us To Sanity."* The belief espoused in Step 2 is spiritual and not just the one based on the senses. The spiritual realm is non-physical, invisible, vast, and unlimited. It is the realm of the unknown, the unfamiliar, where the impossible becomes possible. It is the field where all potential and opportunities exist. The known and familiar self-effort you have been using to get sober belongs to the five senses' limited field.

Therefore, the solution to powerlessness and your addiction problem is not in what you already know but in what you come to believe. You may know something without believing it in your heart. You may know something and doubt whether it works for you. You may know something and fear that it's too hard and challenging for you. If what you know was the answer, you would have stopped drinking and stayed sober many years ago. You may say that you know a lot, but that knowledge has not changed your life in the desired direction. Your life is not where you want it because the knowledge you possess has not been helpful so far. What you come to believe implies developing new beliefs to replace the old and limited sense-based beliefs. You believed in alcohol because you could see the beer, smell it, taste it, feel it, and drink it. Spiritual believing requires you to see the invisible, believe the unbelievable, expect the unexpected, experience, and witness the impossible, trust the unknown. This is the realm of the greater power, Higher Power: God.

Believing in a Greater Power

Higher Power is higher and greater than your limited five senses. You need to believe in a greater power because your five senses are too inadequate to overcome alcoholism. Your belief in alcohol should get less and weaker while you come to believe more and stronger in a Higher Power to experience long-lasting sobriety. The less you believe in a Greater Power, the less the changes and the shorter the time of your sobriety. The weaker you believe, the shorter the duration of your desired changes.

The more you hold on to your old beliefs about alcohol, the more you stay the same, and of course, relapse will be your constant companion.

When you are going through difficult life situations, you want help from a source that can deliver you and rescue you all the time and not sometimes. Alcohol helped you sometimes, and the relief was only temporary, with many adverse side effects. You sought the help of alcohol and drugs to deal with whatever you were going through, but you paid a hefty price to access that help. How long do you want to continue to rely on what is unreliable? How long do you want to continue to depend on what is undependable? How long do you want to continue to trust in what is untrustworthy?

It is helpful to consider the characteristics and abilities of God or Higher Power to which you can avail yourself to solve the problem of powerlessness. A significant consideration to hold as you work toward sobriety with your Higher Power is that God is always available 24/7, always present wherever you are and whatever you are doing. God works with you as you are; there are no deals to be made or special qualifications needed. God never goes to sleep or on summer vacation; you don't have to pay any dues or stand in a line for your turn; you don't have to make appointments or wait for the 'God store' to open so you can go in and get your stuff early in the morning. Other important considerations that you should reflect on daily are that the Higher Power is helpful, dependable, honest, powerful, all-knowing, all-seeing, caring, compassionate, and all present everywhere.

Alcohol and drugs couldn't provide these healing and liberating qualities. You looked to alcohol for inner peace and good life but only got short-lived bliss and many regrets. Believe in something stronger, more significant, and more powerful than alcohol and drugs.

You may ask yourself why you couldn't stop drinking and why you tried everything, but nothing worked.

Predominant and Recurrent Beliefs of the Alcohol and Drug Abuser

Sometimes people come for treatment and reporting that they are sick and tired of being sick and tired. They often present themselves as weak, defeated, exhausted, hopeless, and helpless. They don't know why they can't stop drinking and using drugs because it's no longer fun. They often state and believe that they have tried everything, but nothing worked, and they are on the point of despair. The only sure thing for most of them is that they will continue using drugs and alcohol, with disastrous consequences if they don't get help. They know that obnoxious substances' continued use means three scary options: hospital, jail, or death.

To gain insight into why you kept using alcohol and drugs when doing so was no longer enjoyable, go no farther than your predominant daily and recurrent thought patterns pertaining to alcohol and drugs. Human beings create things and experiences from their thoughts and feelings. Success comes from your beliefs, thoughts, and feelings, and so does failure. Failure thought patterns would not give you success. Stinking thinking will not get you to sobriety. Your failure to stop drinking can be traced to your thoughts and feelings. Become familiar with your own prevalent, continuous, and consistent self-deceptive beliefs and thought patterns. These powerful and regular self-defeating belief patterns are often accompanied by a weak desire to quit entirely and a very feeble non-committal effort to be free from alcohol and drugs.

Below are some common beliefs that alcoholics and drug addicts are usually preoccupied with:

You don't want to run out, so you better hunt early for the drug or drink. You are always planning where you can hide it. You don't want to be caught again today. You figure out what lies you can tell today or this time to get cash. You think you can buy your alcohol since your family will not notice because you are doing an excellent job of hiding it. You are convinced that they won't even detect the smell on your breath.

You can't wait to get home so you can continue to use alcohol and drugs. You keep watching the clock so you can know when to use alcohol and drugs. You spend hours thinking and scheming about what excuse you can give today or this time to avoid family interactions or gatherings. You spend a lot of hours thinking tomorrow you will stop using drugs and alcohol. You always think about where to steal money today. You feel terrible about lying and stealing, but you continue doing them, anyway.

You tell yourself, it's not that bad. It's just snorting heroin or just drinking alcohol. You are not running with the big dogs who do robbery, prostitution, and other ugly stuff. You just need a bag or just a few drinks to get rid of the sickness, but always end up using and taking more than you intended.

You use drugs and alcohol early in the morning to improve an already bad day, which does not get better despite the early start. You try to take prescribed pills the right way without success day after day.

You think alcohol will help you cope with life, even if all the evidence points to the contrary. You hope your family members will not lecture you again today about it. You wonder, can they smell it on you today? How can you avoid being caught by your spouse today? You lie to yourself that you can do it right today and take the medication as prescribed, but that rarely happens.

You believe that using drugs and alcohol helps you experience a rare insight into your situation. Using drugs and alcohol makes you confident and energized. It makes you funny and more comfortable to be around. Using drugs and alcohol makes you more open, outgoing, and sociable.

Using drugs and alcohol makes you feel witty, wiser, and smarter, even with slurred speech. Using the intoxicating stuff helps you get relief from pain, emotional, and physical.
You believe that using harmful stuff hurts nobody. Using drugs and alcohol makes you enjoy things better. Have fun. Your problems go away. You believe you can stop whenever you want to. You use alcohol and drugs to reward yourself, to celebrate both

achievements and non-achievements. To numb yourself and escape depression, fear, anxiety, sadness, etc.

You think you are drinking to cope with uncaring family members. You honestly believe that people like you better when you drink. You use drugs and alcohol to disengage or disconnect from work issues. Whatever you did last night wasn't your fault because you remember nothing.

Using drugs and alcohol makes you have something in common with your friends, more acceptable and fitting in with the crowd.

You can't get through the day without your fix. Using drugs and alcohol makes problems go away; you don't have to worry about them now. Using drugs and alcohol makes bad things not so bad.

Drugs and alcohol make you forget everything. Drinking is acceptable. All grown-ups drink. Drinking makes you feel as good as everybody else.

Your predominant and recurrent belief patterns help to make you sink deeper and deeper into alcoholism. As you can see from the above list, such beliefs are powerful and ingrained in you; you may not be aware of them. They are so powerful that drinking and drug-pushing behavior becomes automatic. You don't have to figure out anything when you want to drink. People become what they think and believe. You are what you think. It's impossible to be sober when your predominant daily beliefs are tilted in favor of alcohol and drugs.

These beliefs will not disappear because you have been sober for a few days, weeks, or months. Addiction beliefs are always alive and active until they are removed and replaced by new ones. Go inside and replace them with new ones. Continuous sobriety comes from sustained and consistently substantial new beliefs. You may fall but stand up and keep moving. Don't give up. The solution is inside you. Alcohol worked so well because you had an unwavering strong faith in it. You had a powerful bond with alcohol because you believe it, trusted it, relied on it, and had confidence in it.

Paradigm Shift

Some alcoholics get sober but do not work on changing their beliefs and are shocked when they relapse. Old and new beliefs cannot exist together in harmony because the old ones are stronger, more powerful, and ingrained as your habits. Years of thinking, believing, and taking alcohol do not easily go away just because you have been sober. Paradigms are rigidly established, stubborn, and ongoing unwritten rules that direct and govern your behavior. You have an ingrained system of beliefs, ideas, values, attitudes, and habits of seeing the world.

Social science has established that a part of the growing process involves gaining and developing memorized, automatic behaviors and emotional responses that define each individual as a personality. As a person grows older, 95% of who you are is in a set of memorized programs (in the body and subconscious mind). Over time, the growing person becomes so familiar with himself/herself that automatic (often undesirable) thoughts go unnoticed.

Emotional Addictions

Automatic emotional reactions and behaviors become part of your personality. Some memorized emotions drive addictive behavior behind every addiction, such as being hooked on drugs, alcohol, gambling, sex, and shopping. Thinking and feeling the same negative way over many years makes you chronically unhappy, lonely, bored, anxious, depressed, bitter, angry, miserable, or physically unwell. You may use past events in your life to validate and justify your memorized negative emotions that have become part of who you are. Human beings tend to hide their fears, insecurities, and weaknesses from others. Change becomes a genuine struggle because you try to work out a solution with the same mind that created the problem. It is almost impossible to solve your problems while you continue to live by past emotions. Looking at the awful experience and reliving the event that caused the problem initially will only serve you by re-arousing the old painful emotions, giving you a potent reason to feel the same negative and painful way.

You will analyze your life by figuring a way out with the same framework of the mind that created it. You will argue for your limitations and find excuses for not changing. In short, the framework of mind that created alcohol addiction cannot help you be sober. The way out of emotional addictions is to unlearn your limiting beliefs and emotions. Freedom comes from confronting your true self and bringing out those fears and weaknesses to your awareness. Identify and make a list of the negative and self-defeating aspects and replace them with positive beliefs and traits. Self-observation, awareness, and acceptance are critical skills for a significant change of self. Observe and realize negative emotional states that have had a considerable impact on your life. Identify and recognize aspects of your personality that drive your thoughts and automatic addiction behaviors. Use your powers of observation to unlearn the negative emotional states. Do constant self-observation and self-awareness so that no emotion, no subconscious behavior, or automatic habit goes without your notice.

Case History of Lonestart

Practical Exercise

Old Beliefs: The story of Lonestart

Question: What did you think, feel, and believe about alcohol when you were taking it?

"I believed alcohol would make me feel better and am happier when I am drunk. I open up to people and connect more easily when intoxicated. Alcohol lets me forget about my worries and troubles because it allows me to relax immediately. I love that it takes away my mental and physical pain, but I have to keep my fingers crossed, hoping this time will be different, and I will stop quickly. I believe alcohol is a family curse; we are doomed to be drunks. It is a portable mental vacation for me. I deserve to drink occasionally because I work

so hard and have little to which to look forward. My attitude is that alcohol makes social gatherings more palatable and fun. I could probably stop after one night of binging. My hands feel so empty when I'm the only one without a drink, and I feel awkward when I am the only one who is sober."

Practical Exercise

New Beliefs: The New Story of Lonestart

Question: What should you think and believe about alcohol and drugs now that you want to be clean and sober?

I want to be sober, and I can never control my drinking. I can never stop at one or two drinks consistently. Alcohol will only make my situation worse in the long run. Drinking makes me an irresponsible mother and deceitful wife, causing me a lot of guilt and shame. I like myself when I am sober, and I become someone I despise when I drink. I want to be healthy. Alcohol is not suitable for my mind and body. The only relief alcohol gives me is very temporary and seductive. Its damaging consequences are far-reaching and long-lasting. Realistically, alcohol isn't fun, and even if it were, it wouldn't mean anything because I never remember a thing.

Alcohol prevents me from being the lady I want to be, and it blocks me from achieving my goals. Drinking will only lead to emotional, physical, social, and spiritual pain. I must stop this. When I drink, I'm a nasty person which robs me of the connections with family and friends. I am allergic to alcohol, and it has robbed me of the life I worked so hard to build. I don't have to drink because I desire to live a life that reflects my values. I cannot drink if I want to be the wife and mom that my family deserves. Alcohol is deadly. I never know if the next drink is my last one.

Mind-Body Connection

Every time you think, the brain produces a chemical that immediately signals the body, telling it to feel exactly the same way the mind is thinking. Great, unlimited happy thoughts produce chemicals that make you feel happy, uplifted and sound. If you have negative, self-defeating thoughts, you produce chemicals that make you feel bad, down, and unhappy. If you have an insecure thought, you also feel insecure. If you have fear thoughts, you also felt fearful. The moment you feel insecure, you also think the way you feel, leading to more chemicals, so you continue to feel how you are thinking and thinking the way you are feeling. You get caught up in this cycle of thinking and feeling, resulting in feeling becoming the means of thinking.

When your thoughts are based on how you feel, the mind is now immersed in the body. You are no longer thinking as a conscious being. You are now thinking as the body because the body is determining the outcome based on feelings. Your feelings and not rational thinking guide your perceptions, choices, and behaviors. How much rational thinking did you put into drinking alcohol? Your state of being consists of what you think and how you feel. As your addiction progressed, there came a time when you couldn't think any other way besides the way you felt. You woke up in the morning feeling bad, and you started thinking bad. You felt terrible and spent the entire day perceiving things from the way you felt. The body should be a servant to the mind, but when you think based on how you feel, the mind becomes the servant to the body. Now the body tells you that you need a drink, or it's okay to have a drug.

The moment you felt the way you think because the brain is in constant contact with the body, you think how you feel and produce more chemicals to feel the way you think and think the way you feel. This cycle of thinking and feeling, feeling and thinking conditions the body to memorize habitual patterns and behaviors better than the conscious mind. When the brain keeps signaling the body in the same way or with the same messages, the body becomes the mind, and the body knows better than the brain.

For example, you may not consciously recall a phone number, but you pick up the receiver, and your fingers dial the number. How does that happen? You can't consciously remember the ten-digit telephone number with your mind, but if you practice it so often, it's your body that remembers the number better than your mind. How many times did you drive and got home safely but could not remember how you got home? Who drove you home on those occasions when you blacked out while sitting behind the wheel? That is how habits and behaviors work.

You may consciously want to change and seriously declare that you want to be sober. Still, you have conditioned your body to be unhappy, unhealthy, guilty, hostile, or fearful and to depend on alcohol for relief over the years. Your conscious mind wants a new life, but your subconscious mind (the body) is used and addicted to the hormones of stress cooled down by alcohol. When the mind and the body are working in opposition, there can never be change, especially when the body becomes the mind. Successful change demands you think greater than how you feel and think greater than the body's memorized emotions.

Two Case Histories Are Presented Below

Old Beliefs: The story of TipsMe

Question: What did you think, feel, and believe about alcohol when you were taking it?

> I was happier and wasn't hurting anyone but myself. I believed no one would find out. I was convinced that God wasn't taking the obsession from me, so I'll just do whatever I want. I felt entitled because I have had so much trauma in my life that I deserved this escape from reality.
>
> My life sucks, so who cares. I'm just going to take a couple of hits---spend just $20, and that's it. I realize how miserable it is to be broke so that I

won't blow all my money this month. If my 20-year-old son talked to me again, I would stop.

Stealing, lying, cheating, and getting away with it was cool on my part. The life of drinking feels normal to me. Responsible and productive members of society were all snobs and judgmental.

I will not get killed or die by crack—that could never happen to me.

New Beliefs: The New Story of TipsMe

Question: What should you think and believe about alcohol and drugs now that you want to be clean and sober?

I ruined my life and have no control when I start. I can't continue to think that I can just do a little bit and stop. The thought of being drunk makes me fearful and paranoid. All my money is gone by the 5th day of the month, and I am going nowhere in my life. I lost my son and two daughters' love and respect, and I must earn it back. People cut me out or completely distance themselves from me. I am the problem and not them. No one trusts me, and I don't trust myself either.

It keeps getting worse and not better. I am not having fun or relaxing — this is wasting away my life. My family worries sick about me, and I must start caring. I am doing things that I would never normally do, and this must stop.

Death or serious injury can and will happen to me if I continue to use drugs and alcohol. Crack will end up killing me. I will die if I continue smoking crack. I will lie there all night tossing and turning with unbearable anxiety, fear, and racing thoughts. I will never have a relationship with my two daughters and son. That makes me nervous. It scares me. I will continue to hate myself and regret causing more guilt and shame.

Old Beliefs: The Story of FixMe

Question: What did you think, feel, and believe about alcohol when you were taking alcohol?

I believed I was in my happy place, I felt happy, but I was lost in reality, trying to do drugs to hide the pain. I thought I wasn't hurting anyone. I thought it would make me a better fiancée and even a better-looking person. In my active disease, my sick brain told me it would help me feel better. I called it liquid courage. I embraced the lies. It made me say and do things outside of what I knew was okay for me to do. Honesty flew out the window. I thought I looked good and behaved great. At the end of my active drinking, I yearned for literal death—selfishness and caring for no one outside of my bottle. I allowed alcohol to rape my soul and spirit. I believed it helped me to fit in, to be socially and sexually attractive. It made me feel confident, and that I had better ideas, and that everything was under control.

New Beliefs: The New Story of FixMe

Question: What should you think and believe about alcohol and drugs now that you want to be clean and sober?

> *I believe I can never drink safely, ever again. I can be sober and relaxed at home. I can be intimate with my spouse without drinking. I can have conversations and be myself with friends and family without drinking. I am physically and mentally healthy, and I do not need alcohol to function. I can enjoy myself doing outside activities without drinking. I can deal with my emotions, good or bad, using healthy coping skills without doing drugs or alcohol. I am a good smart person, and I don't need drugs and alcohol to live my daily life. I can follow my doctor's orders and will take my meds as prescribed daily. I can relax at night, go to sleep, and stay asleep without drugs or alcohol. I can and will enjoy family functions, be a part of my family without drinking and drugging. I can attend and enjoy church instead of staying at home to drink. Getting sober is not enough for me. I am completely and utterly powerless over alcohol. I can never use alcohol and drugs safely. I have to stay on my new thinking and beliefs about alcohol. Drugs and alcohol consumed my life, my finances, my family, and my health.*

To stay sober, break up old patterns that engineered your drug and alcohol lifestyle; otherwise, they will always pull you back to alcohol and drugs. These automatic beliefs and perceptions have always been running the show behind the scenes, with or without your conscious awareness. Sobriety

88

requires seeing the world in a new light, how you see the world when drinking cannot help you stay sober. You need fresh information and new beliefs to experience a new life. There is a need for a paradigm shift whereby your usual way of thinking about alcohol and drugs is replaced by a radically new and different set of beliefs and habits. Reprogram your mind by identifying habitual beliefs and thought patterns associated with drinking, bringing them to the surface, and then replacing them with new ones that will help you stay sober.

What were some of your beliefs about alcohol and drugs when you were using them? Can any of these beliefs help you stay sober? Hopefully, you are getting convinced of the critical importance of changing what you believe. You have to believe differently to have a new life. You have to accurately understand where you are to see the alternative lifestyles that have always been available all these years. If you don't fully comprehend where you are now, you may not see the alternative choices. Where are you now in your thoughts and beliefs about alcohol and drugs?

Practical Exercise

Your Predominant and Recurrent Thought Patterns While Using Drugs and Alcohol

What were your predominant and recurrent thought patterns about alcohol and drugs while you were using them? To benefit from this exercise, be specific and detailed in coming up with your list. You can use items from the list above that you identify with and to relate. Your answers to this question will help you gain insight into why you continued to use drugs and alcohol even when it was no longer fun and exciting to do so.

Restore Us to Sanity

Rarely do people who do drugs and alcohol consider themselves to be insane. They are likely to feel offended, argue, and cuss if labeled as such. A typical way of thinking among alcoholics runs something like this:

"I am different; alcohol does not affect me like other people. I am not one of them. They cannot handle their booze. I can enjoy my book more if I smoke a joint. Then I would re-read one page over five times and give up after several failed attempts. I would do it again the next day, hoping it works this time. It never worked, and I never completed reading any book."

Behaviors and habits unacceptable to the rest of society are considered normal and standard practices among people who use drugs and alcohol. Here is another example of insanity patterns:

I kept telling myself that today I will take the meds as prescribed but always ended up taking double or more sometimes. I used meds for thirty days in less than two weeks. I would agree with family members on the number of drinks but always drank more than agreed. They were unfair to me. I saw nothing wrong with my alcohol. I told myself that I would clean the house better this time with some alcohol, but the house never got cleaned. Every time I completed treatment, I was convinced that now I can control my drug habit and went back to using soon after discharge. It never worked, and treatment did work because I could now use drugs safely after treatment.

Step 2 of Alcoholic Anonymous states that "We came to believe that a power greater than ourselves could restore us to sanity." What is insanity? How were you insane when you were partaking in alcohol and drugs? The standard definition of insanity is doing the same things over and over and expecting different results. It is believing a lie and living a lie. Unfortunately, these are lies you tell yourself daily and not somebody else. Below are some case examples of insanity.

Question: In what specific ways were you insane while drinking alcohol and doing drugs?

What Did You Do?	What Did You Expect?	Actual Result
Went out one night to have drinks	Expected to be home in an hour or two	Woke up behind an ice machine at a gas station; it was in the morning
Went after work to have beers	To stop after a few and go home.	I got accused of messing with a guy's girlfriend. Big fight. Swollen, bloodied face. Costly stitches.
Spent the weekend drinking and watching football with friends	To go back to the Navy base.	A friend took me to the bus terminal, got onto the wrong bus, and headed to Florida and not Atlanta.

Went to ride snowmobiles and have some drinks	Have a great time.	Fell off my snowmobile a few times.
I went to the bar to drink with a friend who gave me a ride home afterward.	To get home safely and have a good night's sleep.	Door keys dropped in the snow. I couldn't get in, so I chopped down the door. I woke up freezing and didn't know what happened.
I went to a picnic, drank beer, and smoked a little pot while riding on motorcycles.	Have a great time.	I ran off the road and spent the night in the hospital.
Drove car high while on prescription drugs, plus alcohol.	To drive home safely and do housework.	I had a terrible accident on the way home. Pills spilled all over. I got pissed at people who were trying to help me.
I drank and took Xanax just before church service.	To relax and chill out in church.	My family noticed the smell and puffed up face, and I had to leave church service.
Drank a lot before picking daughter and friends up.	To get high, have fun, relax, and nobody to notice.	I was passed out on the floor. Family scared I was dead. I spent the day in the ER and not on vacation.
Birthday treats just after work. I took Xanax and some wine while waiting for the family to get home to have dinner.	To celebrate, relax, and feel good on my special day.	I blacked out for the entire weekend.

I stayed home while my family went to church. I was going to watch the service online while drinking.	Drink and be okay by the time they got home.	I passed out on the floor. When they got home and were hurt some more, but that meant nothing to me.
Out drinking with work friends and drank way too much.	Enjoy myself and drive home safely.	I don't remember how I got home and parked my car in my neighbor's garage, thinking it was mine. Felt foolish and useless the next day.
Drinking and doing vast amounts of opiates for over three years daily.	Be normal, functional, and healthy.	Repulsive, unhealthy fatty-looking body. Self-loathing, desiring more alcohol and drugs to cure dysfunctional life.

Insanity: Locked Myself Out of the House

I went to sleep very drunk one night and woke up around 2 a.m. I drank because I could not go back to sleep. I drank one, and there was no open wine bottle in the house. I feared waking up my wife by opening a fresh bottle, and that was when I recalled I had some beers in my outside carpentry workshop attached to the house. I quietly closed the house on my way out to the beer in the workshop. I finished the few beers and tried to get back into the house, but realized that I had locked myself out. I was not prepared to arouse my wife from her sleep and ask her to let me in and explain what I was doing outside in the early morning hours. I had to endure the longest 2 hours of my life until the milk and newspaper delivery arrived. Then I knocked on the door, telling my wife I was collecting the morning deliveries when I accidentally locked myself out. I was back into more drinking, even after such a close shave incident.

Insanity: Passed Out on a Plane

Coming back from a business trip, I boarded a plane early in the morning for a two-hour flight journey home. I had been drinking the previous night with some friends and business partners and also had a few shots at the airport just before the flight. I got onto my seat and immediately fell asleep before take-off, only to be woken up by airline staff telling me it was time to disembark in what seemed like just a few minutes. I thought there must be a mechanical fault, and they wanted us to leave the plane while they repaired it. So, I told the flight attendant that I would just stay on board if that were ok with her. She then told me we had already arrived in London. I had passed out the entire journey and couldn't recall both take-off and landing. When I arrived home, I continued to drink to shake off the exhaustion from this business trip. Everything looked normal to me.

Insanity: I Was Always the First Customer of the Day

There came a time when I needed to start my day with some shots of Vodka. I drank all I had the previous night, which required me to get to the store to get some. Beer sales start at 6 am in my county, so I would patiently wait for the liquor store to open, and I would walk in at precisely 6:05 am to buy enough to last me the whole day. The store employees knew me well because I had done this many times. I didn't want them to think that I drank too much, so I would tell them I was going fishing first and then returning to work in my garden. In reality, I had neither gardened nor did I do any fishing. Neither did I have a yard because I lived in a high-rise apartment complex. Every time I drank early, I knew I wouldn't accomplish anything that day other than sleep in the afternoon and annoying my wife. The next day, it was the same pattern, and I expected things would get better and that I would start drinking in a controlled and responsible manner. That never happened; instead, my drinking got worse, and my wife left me.

CHAPTER FIVE

Breaking the Habit of Being Yourself

Long-term sobriety depends on your decision to turn over your will and your life to the care of the God of your own understanding. This may be a challenging and difficult proposal for some people. Such resistance may come from falsely believing that you were in control and in charge of your life all along. The reality is that you had given over your will and your life to the care of drugs and alcohol. You were no longer in control; alcohol was. You were no longer in charge; your drug of choice was. This is a turning point where you have to make a clear decision about how you will live your life from this point forward. There are several choices from which to pick. You can try to change and stay sober, depending on yourself (5 senses).

The second choice is to continue depending on alcohol, hoping that you will drink moderately one day. The third choice is to develop a relationship with and surrender to God, the Higher Power. The choice is yours. Many people in treatment programs are struggling to stay sober because they have not decided to cut ties with alcohol, hoping that, somehow, they will be able to control their drinking based on self-knowledge and their own smartness.

The Role of the Self on Your Way to the Bottom

What is the self, and why do you have to give up self-will? In the addiction context, the self is best described as *"I want what I want now irrespective of the costs or consequences."* You always drank, even when all the odds were stacked against you. You always managed or forced your way on things, situations, and people against their will and interests.

According to Alcoholic Anonymous or the Big Book of AA, the principal source of trouble for the alcoholic is selfishness and self-centeredness. The book also states that alcoholics are driven *by fear, self-delusion mixed with self-pity to hurt their innocent loved ones without reason, forcing them to retaliate.* Here, I invite you to revisit your decisions, choices, and actions when using alcohol and drugs. Most of those choices you made were within a framework of selfishness and self-deception driven by fear, resentment, self-seeking, and pressure for immediate self-gratification. Life motivated by *"I want what I want when I want it"* can hardly be successful.

There is a very high inclination toward being mean, egocentric, dishonest, impatient, intolerant, and impulsive. Selfishness is a lack of consideration for others. It is being concerned mainly by one's personal gain, profit, or pleasure. A selfish and dishonest person always places himself in a position to be hurt and to conflict with himself and others. Then, when things don't go his/her way, he/she becomes indignant and blames everyone else except himself. A self-centered person creates problems for himself/herself and blames other people for the mess. You want the entire world to see how you feel, but you don't care about anyone's feelings. Egocentrism is the inability to view things any other way except your way. It's your way or no way at all. An egocentric person has inconsistencies between the standards that apply to himself and expects others to adhere to those he/she won't.

An egocentric and self-centered person knows the difference between right and wrong but consistently chooses the wrong with no hesitation.

A self-centered person is excessively preoccupied with himself/herself and his/her own needs. It is all about *"me, me, me."* Such a person thinks only about himself, his desires, needs, and interests while ignoring others, especially those of his/her loved ones.

A self-seeking person is obsessed with the self, self-absorbed, inconsiderate, thoughtless, unthinking, and motivated by his/her advantage without regard for others. He/she is consumed by his/her selfish interests and welfare, to the complete disregard of others. Such a person is excessively conceited and preoccupied with his/her own life and circumstances while being very disinterested in others' well-being, especially those of his/her loved ones. To a self-seeking person, it doesn't matter how others feel because it's all about you. A major worry of the selfish person is *"when will the rest of the world stop misbehaving and start behaving"* so he can be happy. The self has failed and must be given up, or else you continue drinking and doing drugs, driven by selfish, self-centered, and self-seeking behavior. Below are some real-life examples of selfish and self-centered behavior displayed by alcohol and drug addicts:

Task: Write a list of actions you knew to be wrong and inappropriate but did them, anyway. Compare your list with the list below:

- Stole pain medication from grandma and failed employment drug test.

- Used family money on drugs and alcohol instead of bills and food.

- Neglected to take care of my kids; suffered from lost love and respect, but continued drinking alcohol.

- Ignored family concerns about my alcohol and drug abuse and hurt them again and again.

- Offered sex for drugs. Felt wrong, guilt and shame, but I did it again, anyway. I was unfaithful to my spouse; what I wanted was more important than the marriage. My spouse was hurt, furious, angry, and disappointed, but I didn't care. My drugs were a priority.

- Made promises that I knew I would never fulfill— canceled important family invitations at the very last minute.

- Let things pile up: laundry, house bills, dishes. I ignored hygiene by looking for the cleanest among my dirty clothes.

- Was not present in my marriage; was emotionally distant from loved ones, pretended spouse didn't exist. Isolated avoided and pushed away loved ones. I continued to engage in humiliating and self-degrading habits, with utter disregard for the devastating impact on my family.

The self that has been described in the above examples is the one that must be given up to the care of the God of your own understanding. It is an exchange program in that you give up dishonesty for honesty, selfishness for selflessness, impatience for patience, untrustworthiness for trust, no consideration for consideration, self-centeredness for caring, and concern for others, from self-seeking to seeking opportunities to being of service to your life and your community.

That you have stopped drugs, and alcohol does not automatically make you humble, honest, tolerant, and patient. If you have been selfish and self-centered for many years, these negative habits will not go away independently. They will not disappear just because you have stopped drinking for a few days. People in recovery usually believe that all they need is to stop drinking, and all will be well. That is utopia. Being sober is not enough; you have to work at humility, tolerance, patience, and honesty. You cannot eliminate selfishness by wishing it away or by using your power. You need God's help. If you could do it on your own, you would have stopped using drugs and alcohol and lived many sober years back. Have God do for you what you cannot do for yourself.

Question: In what specific ways were you selfish, self-centered, and self-seeking when you were doing alcohol and drugs? Describe specific incidents of the manifestation of self and self-will when you were doing alcohol and drugs.

What is Decision-Making?/Turning Point?

What is decision-making? What was the quality of your decisions when you were drinking and using drugs? So far, you have worked on several critical issues regarding problem definition and identifying the solution. The problem of alcoholism is powerlessness, and the solution is believing in a greater power. You now have to decide where you will get the power and stay connected to that power source. You need a power that will enable you to stop drugs and alcohol and stay sober. The power of alcohol and drugs has let you down all these years. Your own power has sometimes helped you to stop for temporary periods but has not enabled you to stay sober in the long term. This is a major turning point that requires sound decision-making. 'Business as usual' will not work.

How did you make decisions when you were using alcohol and drugs? How was the quality of those decisions? How were your daily decisions to do alcohol and drugs? On what considerations were those decisions based? How proud were you about those decisions then, and how proud are you now? How wise do you feel?

Your feelings and the urgent need to feel different drove most decisions to use drugs and alcohol. Feelings affect both the quality of decisions and the speed at which it makes the decisions. According to neuroscientist and author Dr. Joe Dispensa, thoughts are the language of the mind, and feelings are the language of the body. Decisions to drink alcohol or use drugs were almost invariably based on feelings to please the body while ignoring the consequences.

Short-term goals dictated them to pacify the body at the expense of long-term wellness and wellbeing in all aspects of life. Emotions such as anger, fear, frustration, boredom, and loneliness can lead you to be impatient and rash. Excitement may lead to hasty decisions made without regard to the prevailing facts and implications. In the alcoholic and drug addict's word, desirable standard practices such as using common sense, considering the facts, or thinking before acting don't seem to fit. The body knows no logic and has no commonsense platform. No alcoholic leaves home and says, *"I am going to drink and will sleep in jail tonight for DUI."* No drug addict says, *"I will use all the money I have so that I become homeless and sleep under a bridge."* No spouse continues to use drugs and says, *"I will use drugs until I have destroyed my life, hurt my children, and ruined my marriage."* No one goes to drink and say, *"I am going to drink tonight so that tomorrow I can lose my job and become a beggar in the streets."* Guilt, shame, and regrets are ever-present because daily decisions based on feelings don't see consequences and consider nothing outside the present feeling. The body or your subconscious mind operates on conditioned programs driven by feelings and addictive habits.

There is a need for thoughts to filter emotions and sanction acceptable actions and behaviors. Self-discipline is the ability to subdue your flesh, to act on thoughts and not emotions. Greatness is the ability to think more significant than how you feel. We base sound decisions on facts. Daily decisions to drink and use drugs ignore the facts, which lead to undesirable results and regrets.

The facts you have gathered so far from work in the previous chapters are:

Fact 1:

You are an abnormal drinker, and you can never drink safely. The more you drink, the worse your condition deteriorates.

Fact 2:

You have a problem whose nature and intensity have been unclear all along.

Fact 3:

The problem has symptoms and dealing with them does not get rid of the underlying condition.

Fact 4:

The problem is powerlessness over alcohol, and you still have power in other areas of your life.

Fact 5:

Powerlessness has incredibly damaging consequences on your mind, body, and spirit, including other essential components of life such as health, relationships, finances, career, and hobbies that you may not have taken into account.

Fact 6:

Your efforts to solve the problem have not worked. Everything you have tried so far has not helped you to stay sober. Since the self has failed, you need a more viable solution to avoid the hospital (institution), prison, or death.

Fact 7:

The right solution is beyond your five senses and intellectual faculties, hence the need to believe in and surrender to a Greater Power.

Fact 8:

There is a need to be rescued from the insanity of falling in the same ditch day after day, with your eyes open.

Now that you have assembled the facts about your alcoholic condition, the conclusion is that what you need is power, and you get that power by believing in a power higher and greater than your five senses. What exactly do you do when turning over your will and your life to God?

What is Your Will and Your Life?

Successful recovery requires you to give over your will and your life to the care of God of your own understanding. What is self-will? Your will is your thinking, perceptions, feelings, and beliefs. Your life here refers to all of your actions put together. You benefit more from yielding to a greater power than trying to do it your way. Your ways have produced no lasting benefit so far. Over the years, you may have unsuccessfully tried to reduce drinking, moderate it, control it, and even stop it completely. How long do you want to continue failing? How sane is the habit of doing the same drinking and the same drug use day after day but expecting a different outcome?

Your will and life are inside you and are given expression in your beliefs, thoughts, choices, and behaviors. A person's will is his thinking, and the life of a person comprises all his actions put together. Turning *"our will and our lives"* is saying goodbye to your addictive thought patterns and behaviors. You no longer need them because they were fueling the addiction lifestyle. You need new thinking habits that support sobriety. Examples of self-defeating and self-destructive belief patterns are, *"I am in control. I got this. It ain't that bad. I can stop when I want"*. It is not possible to stay sober based on this kind of dishonest thinking. Unfortunately, some people in recovery continue to think the way they are used to and are disappointed when they relapse repeatedly. Step 3 of AA requires you to turn over your will and life to the care of a God of your own understanding. Become a new person in your thinking, feeling, and beliefs.

To Who Are You Turning it Over? Who Are You Surrendering To? (Spirituality Vs. Religion)

How do you feel about letting go of habits you have been practicing for many years? How do you feel about allowing someone or something to exercise control over your life?

People ask, *"How can a God I don't see or understand help me stop drinking and stay sober?"* In their desperation, they create imaginary Higher Powers who are both physical and visible. Stories abound where people have used their dog, a tree, a friend, or a chair as their Higher Power. It is important to point out that spirituality is not the same as being religious. Religion is about strict adherence to beliefs, rules, regulations, and procedures. It is a normal way of doing things, following accepted standards. People born in different religions are raised and expected to respect and obey their religious customs and teachings without question. Such beliefs and expectations are from outside the person. Spirituality is from within.

Spiritual life starts with surrendering, whereby you admit being helpless and that you simply don't know how to resolve the situation. If you knew, you would have been sober long ago. It is essential to remind yourself who you are surrendering to and what you are giving up. Intimate knowledge of who you are surrendering to will make the process easier and smoother. Little knowledge of anything is dangerous. Ignorance is not always bliss.

All these years, you have been turning over your will and your life to untrustworthy, the unreliable and erratic power of alcohol and drugs.

Now you are to yield your thoughts and actions to the Source of Life, the Universal Mind, Universal Intelligence, and Infinite Wisdom, who is all-knowing, all-present, all-powerful, all-loving, compassionate, and always forgiving. You are turning over your life to the Greatest Wisdom, creator, and owner of the entire universe, including the natural and supernatural, the physical and non-physical, the visible and invisible, and of the known and unknown.

Higher Power is the Divine presence in you, around you, all over you, who works for you and with you. God does not live in some place far away from you and beyond your reach. He is always with you in your past, present, and future. You are turning over your life to the power that keeps you breathing and alive in your sleep. He is the Universal Intelligence that wakes you up every morning and has numbered the hairs on your head. He is the one who helps you to drive your car in the middle of the night while you are very drunk and almost unconscious.

You made alcohol your helper and your god when you were drinking it, but it didn't work. Neither did cocaine, marijuana, and heroin. Most, if not all, of your efforts to solve the problem have failed. Now is the time to try something that works. God is already with you and working in your life. How many addicts do you know who are no longer alive because of alcohol and drugs? Yet you are still alive. Is it because you are smarter? God enables your lungs to breathe and your heart to beat. Can you do it with your five senses? You are to turn over life to the one who kept you safe and alive during your frequent visits to violent, crime-ridden, and drug-infested neighborhoods. How did you survive the deadly gunfire wars, the dangerous robberies, and the self-abuse of your body (not eating food for long periods)? You are giving over your will to the one who always protected you, defended you, and loved you, free of charge. You couldn't afford to pay Him, anyway.

Why is Surrendering to God's Higher Power Is Important?

The same mind that created a problem cannot solve the problem. The thought patterns, beliefs, and memorized emotional responses that produced the addiction cannot be relied on to solve the problem. Stop trying to dig a mountain using a teaspoon. That will not work. Narrow addictive thinking and believing created the alcoholic lifestyle, and that same way of thinking cannot take you to sober living. Have you ever wondered why your life has not been changing despite the hard work you put into it? The thoughts you have been having do not give you the answer you have been looking for all these years; they consistently led you to a dead end. The beliefs that you have been having have not given you the sober life that you desire. The actions you have been acting have led you downhill instead of uphill. How much longer are you prepared to keep getting lost and relapsing? Here is your opportunity to change by letting go of limited thinking and addiction-oriented beliefs while you surrender to an unlimited, more generous, and more resourceful power. Surrendering gives you immediate access to the limitless knowledge and bountiful wisdom of God. It is allowing Him to guide and direct you to sober living. After all, everything you have tried of your own volition using your best thinking has not worked out yet. This is an appropriate moment to turn to and stay hooked upon God instead of alcohol and drugs. In its present addictive form, your conscious mind can never get you the answer and can never help you move forward. It thinks, acts, and feels in ways that create more of the same. The result is living in the past instead of moving into a new life of freedom, inner peace, joy, security, and confidence. The all-knowing and wiser Higher Power should help you overcome the limitations and hardships that you created for yourself through your thoughts, beliefs, and perceptions without intention and awareness.

A person who thinks and feels the same way day after day lives in the past and nothing is new there. Without new thinking and new beliefs, you cannot break loose from the ordinary and same old alcohol and drugs life. Have you ever wondered why your life is not changing despite your best efforts to do so? How much longer are you willing to continue living in the past? How much longer are you going to continue tolerating being a slave to alcohol? If you are sick and tired of being a servant to alcohol, maybe this is the best time to let go of the past and embrace the new. God can help you overcome your limitations. You have been relying on alcohol, depending on alcohol, and putting all your trust and confidence in alcohol. Surrendering is placing your reliance, dependence, trust, and confidence in God instead of inanimate and harmful substances.

The surrender option is not the only one. You always have other alternatives at your disposal. One approach which many people in recovery opt for is to continue using drugs and alcohol while hoping that their determination, thinking the same way, believing the same way will one day rescue them from their drinking and drug troubles. The outcome of this option is well-known and predictable, relapse, and failure. The other choice is to initiate contact and keep connected to the Universal Intelligence (God), who possesses unlimited resources, all at your disposal for your use 24/7 and with no price tag. God is more dependable than alcohol and drugs. Quick fixes have not helped, and they will never make you sober. Your alcoholic mind can never see the answer, can never see the solution, and never see the way forward. The proof of such inability is that you have tried to be sober on your own, not once but many times, and failed. When using drugs and alcohol, your mind operates in ways that create more of the same troubled life. Surrendering is deciding to stop living in the past and moving into a new life of sobriety and freedom.

Once you surrender self-will to your Higher Power (God), you must quit trying to do things your way. A narrow focus on alcohol and drugs made it impossible for you to see and experience the available and abundant alternative life options. The uninhibited exercise of your free will and doing things your way impedes God's efforts to free you from living in the past and engaging in the same behaviors day after day while expecting different results. Stop obstructing God by continuing to do what you have been doing. Going back to the same addictive and automatic habits such as selfishness, self-centeredness, impatience, and dishonesty is the worst way to obstruct God's love and help. A business-as-usual approach and trying to stay sober on your own terms does not always work. You gave alcohol and drugs permission to solve your problems, but that didn't work. You have tried your own effort, using your best thinking, but that didn't work either.

Creative Wisdom (God) knows all the potentials and opportunities you may have never thought of or imagined. Limited thinking and memorized emotional responses to life made it impossible for you to see the available and abundant alternative possibilities waiting to be pursued by you. Your free will and doing things your way blocks God's efforts to liberate you from yourself, free you from dwelling in the problem, and protect you from engaging in the same behaviors while expecting different results. You must stop obstructing God by not doing the known, and the familiar failed solutions.

You fight against yourself by surrendering to God and then trying to control the outcome. Don't try pushing and forcing for the desired outcome which is staying alcohol and drug-free. Forcing your way to get what you want might have worked when you were hustling for money, alcohol, and drugs, but that won't work with God. Let go of your thoughts and beliefs about how, when, and in what form the result will appear. Instead, embrace the fact that God is alive, real, and fully aware of your problems, and capable of taking care of all your needs. Surrendering means trusting in a result that you may have never thought of, having confidence in an unknown, unpredictable, but desirable outcome because the all-knowing and loving Intelligence has taken over. Your role is to trust and obey. Lack of trust will produce doubt, fear, impatience, frustration, and the wrong conclusion that God does not want to help you. You are not new to the trust-and-obey game. You trusted and obeyed alcohol and drugs, and you know the results first-hand.

You take God out of the picture when you unknowingly return to unconscious programmed habits: your old ways of doing things, your familiar patterns of perceiving people and the world. It is self-defeating for you to yield self-will to God and still try to control the outcome. Let go and let God take over your life. The way you are used to doing things cannot and has not produced the desired solution so far. Your most recent relapse was known and predictable, although you were shocked and disappointed. When you surrender to God, expect the unexpected, believe the unbelievable, expect the impossible because the unlimited, all-knowing Universal Intelligence (God) has taken over. Previously, alcohol and drugs were in control. They were in charge and responsible for the unusable solutions they provided you since you put your trust in them. After you surrender, that will no longer be the case.

You must understand that the invisible Higher Power (God) knows you, sees you, is fully aware of your life story, and can take care of all your needs and desires. Before embarking on recovery, you trusted alcohol and drugs, you relied on them, but this didn't resolve your life's problems. Alcohol and drugs may have taken temporary care of some of your needs, but they created larger ones. They left you scarred and bruised. Surrendering moves from fear to courage, from doubt to confidence, from unbelief to faith, from hesitation to certainty, from despair to hope, and from frustration to patience.

Surrendering means matching your will to the will of your Higher Power, matching your love of self to the love God has for you, and matching your thoughts to the thoughts of Universal Mind (God). When you see situations and circumstances the same way God sees them, He will answer your call.

When true surrendering has occurred, you must rejoice, feel inspired, grateful, excited, and appreciative because your answer is on the way. Live your days expecting all your prayers have been answered and the assurance that your needs have been completely met. This is spirituality as opposed to sense knowledge, where seeing is believing. There is nothing new in anticipation before the manifestation of what you want. You were doing this when you thought about your drug of choice. You would get excited, animated, and aroused long before you laid your hands on the drug. You would taste the drug in your mouth even before your dealer delivered it. You would salivate before you ingested the drug. When you surrender to your Higher Power, live in the reality that your long-awaited bus to sobriety has arrived. After all, with God, all things are possible, and *"I can do all things through Christ, which strengthens me."*

Very little happens when you view situations your own way that is far removed from how God looks at the same issue. Awareness and acceptance that your prayers have already been answered should take care of the doubt, worry, fear, and frustration commonly associated with unanswered prayer. Doubt means you are not sure that God can do it for you. Fear shows God is unreliable. Worry, impatience, and frustration mean telling God to pick up the pace and stop delaying you but hurry and adjust His timing to yours. When you were on the playing field, you wouldn't be frightened of the bully when you knew that your big brother is around and that He does not take nonsense from any bully. When you surrender to God, you can access someone more incredible and more powerful than a big brother. When you rely on God in place of alcohol, you can stay uplifted and looking forward to the future instead of dreading it, which is always the case when you depend on your limited five senses.

You may consider yourself to be very smart and knowledgeable, but you don't know everything. God does. You may know parts of the way out of your problem, but God knows the complete way. You may have a rough idea of where you are going in your life, but God has already been there. Alcohol does not know inner peace, good health, and a good marriage, but God does. He knows where you are and where you should be. So why not let him guide you? Alcohol and drugs led you to the wrong destination for many years, and you accepted a part in getting lost. Heroin and whisky don't know where you are, and they will keep you where you don't want to be.

Unlike alcohol and drugs, God can lead you out of the dumps to your higher ground. Cut out the guesswork. Stop struggling on your own. God has better help than alcohol and drugs. Alcohol has been the director of your life, with undesirable results. Now is the time to allow your Higher Power to lead you. Your natural thinking and wisdom are very limited. The magic of alcohol has failed you. So what do you do? Go the extra mile guided by the unlimited supernatural wisdom of God. You were looking for this extraordinary and supernatural intervention from alcohol and got some relief. However, the good times were short-lived and often followed by a trail of problems and disappointments. There are no side effects when you allow God to direct your life. Transfer your trust from cocaine to your Higher Power if you want to stay sober. If you could do it on your own, you would not need the help of drugs and alcohol.

God is waiting to help you as soon as you are ready, willing, and obedient. There is nothing new in this proposition because you have been ready for, willing to be ruled by, and obedient to alcohol and drugs all these years. Your willingness and obedience kept you hooked to these substances. The same willingness and obedience will connect you to your Higher Power. Your understanding can wait because your obedience is critical. Do you think you clearly understood alcohol, or you were just being obedient? You drank because you felt like even when you sometimes thought otherwise. That is obedience without understanding. You used to get daily instructions from drugs, and you were very obedient. You obeyed alcohol and drugs without raising a finger but with insufficient understanding. You should now get your daily instructions from a more reliable source, your Higher Power. Don't lead yourself and claim that it's God because that won't work too.

Self-Will Has Failed: Self-Will Did Not Work

An alcoholic and drug addict who genuinely wants to stop using and stay sober can rarely succeed based on self-will and self-knowledge. If the determination was all that you needed for sobriety, you could have stopped drugs and alcohol long before you reached the bottom of the bottom. How much time do you have to continue failing by applying self-will? It is a liability that you have to give up. Surrender it repeatedly in your recovery journey to stay sober. Alcoholics and drug addicts are in the habit of surrendering their self-will at the start of the day, then unknowingly take it back during the rest of the day. An addict may pray and even cry for help from God but bounces back to familiar negative habits, foul moods, and unpleasant attitudes that work against his/her valuable prayer. Every prayer to God is valuable. You are worrying about what you have just prayed for means you doubt whether God can help you. Having anxiety and fear about something you have prayed for shows a lack of trust that God is dependable enough to rescue you. You had no doubts about alcohol and drugs. You had absolute trust in drugs but are hesitant with your Higher Power. What has happened to wisdom and common sense? Praying for help and continuing to do things your own way keeps you in the same place. Nothing changes, other than that your addiction gets worse.

Successful recovery requires a complete surrender of self-will. Cease trying to control the outcome. Quit trying to be your own Higher Power. God does not need an assistant. Surrendering does not mean that you are weak or are a defeated doormat. It is awakening to the reality that we cannot rely on the thoughts and beliefs that created the problem to solve the problem. If that were the case, you would have solved the problem long before it made your life unmanageable.

When you surrender, you are still responsible for making your plans, pursuing your goals, and improving your life. However, this time, your thinking, beliefs, and perceptions are directed by your Higher Power instead of being propelled by alcohol and drugs. Your choices and actions are motivated and guided by God instead of your drug of choice. This change demands shifting from being under the influence of alcohol to being under the inspiration and leadership of your Higher Power. Recognize that alcohol and drugs' leadership has misled you and left you stranded, feeling helpless, and sometimes homeless. The influence of substances works against you and not for you. It pulls you down and not up.

How to be Under the Influence and Direction of Your Higher Power/God

Here we examine the difference between being under the influence of alcohol and being under the inspiration of God:

You are familiar with being under the influence of alcohol and drugs, and the question is how to become under the influence and direction of your Higher Power.

Some people in recovery vehemently dislike and object to giving control over to a Higher Power, invisible and unfamiliar. To such people, Higher Power control is hard, impractical, very difficult, and sometimes just not acceptable. They may have the following questions:

Who is Higher Power, God?

What is He like?

How do I contact and connect with this invisible power?

How do I work with a power I do not see?

How do I know if God/Higher Power is real?

Due to the inability to answer the above questions, some alcoholics continue using their self-will and effort, hoping for a different result. However, what usually happens is an endless pattern of relapses. To the alcoholic and drug-addicted mind, failure and problems of addiction are something else. Through a combination of self-delusion and self-deception, failure looks like being in control, having fun, or just being unlucky sometimes.

To understand how to get under the influence of God, look at how you, day after day, elevated alcohol and drugs to a status of them being your Higher Power. Every alcoholic and drug addict has already surrendered his/her power, authority, independence, and freedom to alcohol and drugs. Although it's all gone, it doesn't look so in his/her addicted brain. He/she holds the false belief that he/she is still in charge. -He/she unknowingly entertains the mistaken idea that he/she is still standing on the carpet and yet the rug was pulled away from under his/her feet many years back.

Below is proof that you had become a prisoner to alcohol and drugs, a kidnap victim, a servant, and a slave.

The addict turned his will and life to alcohol and drugs through the following daily habits (being under the influence):

Thinking about alcohol all the time with satisfaction and a sense of relief from the anticipation of the next one.

Persistently holding the unhealthy belief that alcohol and drugs are helpful, a rescue, an escape, and a source of deliverance, but oblivious to the damaging, shameful, and sometimes embarrassing consequences of substance abuse.

Confusing alcohol and drugs for a dear friend, an unreliable partner whom you trust and depend on anyway, a preferred companion who is always available, a troublesome buddy who is easy to get along with, a confidante who always listens and doesn't argue or talk back.

Being preoccupied with thoughts of obtaining the next high and getting the next drink.

Treating alcohol and drugs as your all-day main focal point, a major priority above work, family, friends, and loved ones.

Put all your thoughts, energy, and zeal into activities centered on alcohol and drugs.

Being more excited, lively, and enthusiastic about alcohol and drugs while being less interested and uninspired by family engagements and other such 'dull' and 'bothersome' issues.

Scrambling to get a drink as soon as you wake up, going next door, or looking for other users if nothing is left from last night.

Figuring out throughout the day how much you have left, who has it, whom you want to share with, and what to do next once you run out.

Being consumed by the desire to save some to help you start your day tomorrow, going to work, and do your work, enjoying the comfort that you will get your fix soon after.

The above list is not exhaustive, and it shows a person who has pawned his/her valuable life to valueless alcohol and drugs. The list shows that rather than the addict being in control, it is the alcohol that has now taken over control of his/her entire life, not just a part of it. You are now under the influence of alcohol. All your decisions, choices, and activities are dictated by alcohol and drugs, which are now in the driver's seat, and you have become an unwilling but cooperative passenger in your car. The name of the car is "Your Life."

Why not become a willing and cooperative passenger in your own life that is driven and guided by your Higher Power? When you lose control of the steering wheel of your life, alcohol and drugs took over, although you, the addict, didn't see it that way. Denial, excuses, blaming, and justification do not take away the fact that you have lost control of the substances. Facts are stubborn. Facts refuse to be covered up by denial. Facts refuse to be silenced by selfishness, dishonesty, irritability, anger, and resentment. No hot argument will demolish the fact that you have lost direction to alcohol and drugs and, therefore, the need to turn over your will and your life to a more helpful and resourceful power which is greater than yourself, greater than alcohol, more powerful than your drug of choice, more reliable than your limited thinking and feeble attempts to solve the addiction problem.

Surrendering to a Higher Power should not be difficult because you had a lot of practice and experience while using drugs and alcohol. Look at your addiction, and you will see a lot of first-hand proof you handed your life over to alcohol and drugs. You become under the influence of God by thinking and interacting with Him continuously and consistently every day, all day. One brief prayer in the morning or before going to bed is inadequate. Sunday service only is also inadequate. If you redirect half or even a quarter of the time, energy, and effort you used on alcohol and drugs toward your Higher Power, you should be able to stay sober. You can experience tremendous results by transferring the excitement and zeal for alcohol and drugs to your Higher Power. To be under the influence of God, do the following; be frequently preoccupied with thoughts of God, persistently hold the belief and expectation that He can help you and rescue you, treat Him as your priority and the main point of focus and not an afterthought, be consumed by the desire to be under His direction, guidance, and presence all the time and not sometimes when you are in trouble, bring to God the same interest, enthusiasm, and excitement that you showed toward alcohol and drugs. If you could do it with alcohol and drugs, you surely can do it better with God.

How to Establish a Relationship with God/Higher Power

Some people develop cold feet when they learn that they have to give over their will and their lives to God in Step 3 of AA. To such people, it makes little sense to rely on an unseen, unknown, and unfamiliar power. They don't know where to start, let alone what exactly to do to work with a Higher Power.

Successful relationships have the following key attributes: love, trust, respect, honesty, commitment, loyalty, active listening and paying attention, patience, etc. Here are some real-life descriptions of how people viewed their relationship with alcohol and drugs during many years of using them, characterized by deep love, devotion, and commitment.

Trust

I had a strong trust for alcohol because it helped me to feel different.

I was very devoted to alcohol; my pillar of support always available.

I had a strong affection for alcohol, thinking about it all day, every day. How much is remaining?

How long will it last? Will I have enough? What to do if I run out or I need to get more.

I looked to alcohol for an escape, for deliverance from everything else going on around me.

Alcohol always created an alternative magical reality, which I couldn't accomplish without it. It created a new world for me, my world, which enabled me to look at people and issues differently.

It took away the tension. Alcohol helped me to relax and stabilize my mood.

Commitment/Loyalty

I was totally committed to alcohol; I gave it my all, my time, my money, my integrity, my dignity, my sanity, and my life.

I was very loyal to alcohol; a big fan of the bottle could hardly go through a day without it. I had to have it wherever and whatever was going on.

I made sure I always have enough money for alcohol. Other more important things in my life could wait, but not dear alcohol. It occupied the top position. The most important asset (liability) I had in my corner was alcohol. That is how it appeared when I was using it.

I pursued alcohol beyond reasonable limits and took many risks, many of them very dangerous, but I didn't care.

Respect

There was no respect between me and alcohol, but I stayed in the disrespectful relationship; I was always on the receiving end. I was always the loser, with short-lived victories, which looked like much at the time. I felt terrible and didn't want to drink some days, but I kept on in this abusive and destructive relationship because it always made me feel different.

I frequently experienced lots of abuse: drunken falls, bruises, injuries, emergency room visits, blackouts, hangovers, morning sickness, memory loss, arrests and jail time, and much more.

Active Listening and Paying Attention

Mary*: "I was severely injured in a car accident and had excruciating pain. The medication was not working. Cocaine, alcohol, and marijuana would take away the pain. The drugs enabled me to take my mind off the pain. They helped me to deal with the trauma, nightmares, and the general apathy of life. Since the pain relief was temporary, I would use it again and again, more and more. This vicious cycle was a daily affair. In reality, all this was an illusion because I was paying a lot of attention to nothing positive. The drugs worsened the original injury problem and brought many more headaches and sleepless nights."*

Pete: "*I would wake up feeling powerful urges to drink, took some, and then took a shower. I had a second one on my way to work. All this looked normal to me when I was doing it. There was nothing unusual, so I took the third one in the car park before going in. This pattern went on every day, all day long. Alcohol helped me to deal with anxiety, although it became worse."*

Gidza*: "Weekends were my me time starting every Friday afternoon. After work out at the gym, I would get a bottle of whisky while watching TV, drink it all, go to the bar, drink some more, and pass out. Saturday was the same. More alcohol from the time I wake up until I passed out again. I* *was consumed and preoccupied with alcohol. Nothing else mattered."*

Jongg: *"As soon as I woke up, I would use some leftovers from the previous night. My dealer would pass by and give me some more. Then I would find ways to make some money to buy more drugs because I would get sick, and my body started shutting out if I stopped using. This went on every day, all day. Using and getting drugs became my full-time occupation."*

As you can deduce from these stories and your personal experience with addiction, you handed your life over to alcohol and drugs, hoping to change how you felt, but that didn't work because it was always a temporary fix, with numerous adverse side effects. Alcohol and drugs have failed you. Relying on drugs has proved unreliable. Why not look for a more robust alternative that will help you resolve your limitations, shortcomings, and character defects effectively? Below are some suggestions on how to arrive at a more useful and practical conception of God as you understand Him:

- ✓ My God is helpful.

- ✓ My God is loving (unconditionally).

- ✓ My God is forgiving.

- ✓ My God is ready and willing.

- ✓ My God is dependable and reliable.

- ✓ My God is honest and trustworthy.

✓ My God is available 24/7 (is all-present, all-knowing, all-powerful).

✓ My God has no favorites.

✓ My God does not stress over what you have been doing.

Developing a close relationship requires the same qualities that you had for alcohol and drugs. These are love for God instead of alcohol, relying on God instead of drugs, depending on God instead of alcohol, trusting in God instead of drugs, having confidence in God instead of alcohol, getting committed to God instead of drugs, showing undivided loyalty to God instead of drugs, respecting God instead of alcohol, listening to God instead of drugs, and paying attention to God instead of alcohol and drugs. Finally, I encourage you to be preoccupied with God and be with your Higher Power wherever you go and whatever you are doing. Let God take the place of alcohol and drugs in your daily life. That is how you can stay connected to Him, gain the power to overcome powerlessness, and stay sober.

Printed in Great Britain
by Amazon

86191801R10079